Secrets, Stories, Skeletons & Stones

Secrets, Stories, Skeletons & Stones

by

Bernard Maitland Balfour

Cranstone House Publishing

First published by
Cranstone House Publishing, 222 King Street, Aberdeen AB2 3BU
March 1993

ISBN 1 898064 00 8

Printed by Waverley Press (Aberdeen) Limited

CONTENTS

FOREWORD

For twenty-five years I had the pleasure of conducting tours, or lecturing to various groups on Local History, during which time I related (and heard) many traditional stories. Some of these tales I was taught at my mother's knee, she herself having a fund of local knowledge, being the daughter of the gallant Aberdeen Sea Beach Rescue, Henry Mitchell.

Over the past decade, a number of people have asked when I would put my talks into book form—well, here's the answer!

I am indebted to the Editor of the "Evening Express" for permission to include some items which have already been published within its pages, and to Charles Riddell, a friend of long-standing, for the generous loan of some of his old postcards; other photographs were kindly supplied by Alan Forrest (Aberdeen Arts and Recreation); Maureen Gorshkov (Tourist Board); Norman Adams (P.P.D.); Jim McDonald (Grampian Transport); Mr Todd (Incorporated Trades); Captain Colin Harrison (Gordon Highlanders Regimental HQ); and Keith Murray (Cranstone House Publishing, Aberdeen); the remaining photographs are by the author. I also record grateful thanks to my wife, Isobel, who supplied the drawings and has been my constant companion on historical fact-finding expeditions for over forty years, and to my late brother, Henry, a fellow-traveller with me on the Local History Trail, for even longer. Thanks to the staff of Waverley Press in general and to Brian Thomson in particular, and finally to Cindy and Bill Anderson for their help and encouragement.

THE SILENT SENTINELS WITH SECRETS IN THEIR HEARTS OF STONE

Many Aberdonians travel along busy Dee Street and never give a second glance at the muckle steen (pictured here) which stands in an alcove at the corner of Dee Street and Langstane Place, opposite Windmill Brae.

The building which houses the stone, the former Watt and Grant's store in Union Street, has changed its role to selling fast foods, but the lang stane is still there giving its name to the area—Langstane Place.

These stones have a history dating back thousands of years. The one in Langstane Place was probably part of a pre-historic stone circle which stood at the top of Windmill Brae—long before the Windmill was ever there.

It is reckoned that there were about 900 of these stone circles in Britain, and about 200 of them were to be found in North-east Scotland. They have been called the silent mysterious symbols of a long forgotten faith.

For ages it was considered unlucky to interfere with such circles and even recently, to avoid any disaster, it was customary to leave one stone undisturbed. But despite this wise precaution, many stone circles were completely destroyed, leaving only a name.

Examples of this can be seen at Hatton o'Cruden, where a farm known as Standing Stones commemorates a circle long since gone. A similar instance is Standing Stones at Monymusk. The names Rathen and Old Rayne also keep tradition alive as they are Gaelic for stone circle.

In the city, as well as at Windmill Brae, there is still a single stone in the grounds of the former Hilton Academy, and there used to be a circle at Hill Street, just above Woolmanhill. Most circles are basically to the same plan—three circles, one inside each other. The individual stones are anything from 4ft-9ft tall, number between 6 and 10, with each stone weighing some five tons.

However, there are exceptions to the basic plan, as in the circle at Cullerlie, near Echt, and at Broomend of Crichie, near Inverurie, which resembles the circle at Avebury near Salisbury, 600 miles south, in having a ditch around it, and in being crossed by an avenue.

Incidentally, in the North-east area we have something peculiar in our stone circles which resembles nothing else in the rest of Britain. This is an immense block of stone—the altar stone—weighing anything up to 20 tons, lying between the two tallest, or flanker, stones. Many of the altar and flanker stones have little hollows or cup marks gouged out of them, which leads imaginative people to suppose blood sacrifices were performed on them by the light of the full moon!

There's no real evidence of what the stone circles were used for, although graves have been discovered in and around many of them.

Whatever their real purpose, there are plenty of theories and stories about stone circles. One Cambridge scientist worked out that the altar stone at Sunhoney, just beyond Echt, is in fact a star chart on which the correct relationships of the principal stars, in the Hercules, Corona, Little and Great Bear constellations are carved.

In addition, the altar stone at Rothiemay, near Huntly, shows the Pole star, the constellations, and the first magnitude stars on its surface!

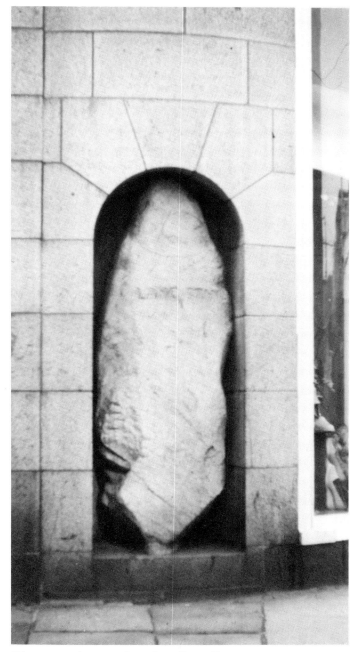

The mysterious and ancient Lang Stane.

Scorning such hypotheses, the good folks of the North-east prefer their own notions regarding the standing stones, especially if they have carvings or symbols on them. One such stone is the Maiden Stone at the Chapel of Garioch—but that's another story for another page!

HEARTBEATS HEARD FROM BEYOND THE GRAVE?

Many names which we think typically Scottish—Stewart, Bruce, Grant, Fraser, Sinclair, Graham and Melville—have nothing to do with Scotland at all, and in fact are of Norman/French origin!

The names belonged to great Norman nobles who came to Scotland in the 13th century at the invitation of David I. These nobles were granted large areas of land on the understanding that they would come to the King's help with a certain number of armed men when needed. In turn, the nobleman sub-divided his land among his knights on the understanding that they would help him. This was the so-called feudal system.

The Norman barons set up castles in the middle of their land. Usually they were made of wood and stood on a little hill. The hill, called a motte, was flat-topped, conical, and made of earth. A good example can be seen in this photograph of the Bass at Inverurie, which occupied a strategic position at the junction of the Rivers Urie and Don.

Although the wooden castles have long gone, the mottes remain at some sites. One can be visited in the Aberdeen area in the grounds of the former Balnagask House.

The land was owned in the 13th century by Cormac de Nug (Nigg), and his castle was well placed to overlook the River Dee and the Bay of Nigg.

Other mottes which have gone but whose sites are remembered are the ones belonging to Gillecoaim, who gave his name to Gilcomston, and Ruadri whose name is commemorated in Ruthrieston.

However, as well as a motte, the Bass at Inverurie also has a graveyard. And buried there is Marjorie Elphinstone. She was married to James Leslie of Upper-boat, Inverurie. Majorie fell ill, took to her bed, and was found by James apparently dead. She was duly buried at the Bass cemetry and her mourning husband went home to the empty house.

Unknown to the mourners, the local gravedigger had seen Marjorie lying in her coffin and had noticed that she was wearing a valuable ring. He waited until darkness had fallen and returned to the grave to open the coffin.

Unable to remove the ring, he began to try to cut it off. The pain woke Marjorie, who had only been in a coma. She climbed out of the coffin, ignoring the amazed grave-robber, and set off home dressed only in her shroud!

James Leslie was sitting at Upper-boat holding a wake as was then the custom. Hearing a knock at the door he exclaimed: "If I hadn't seen Marjorie kisted, I'd sweer that wis her chap!" On opening the door he beheld his late wife standing there. Marjorie in fact outlived her husband and married again!

You can see her grave in the Bass graveyard. In my young days, the story was that she still wasn't dead and if you listened at the gravestone you could hear her heartbeat. I did—and heard a murmuring sound! I'm told that the noise is really an underground spring bubbling on its way to the nearby Urie. But you never know—do you!

The Bass Motte . . . or hill at Inverurie.

THE SKELETON ON THE RIVER DEE

"Nae man can tether time nor tide," wrote Robert Burns in Tam O'Shanter. How true this is in the case of the Shakkin' Briggie, the skeleton of which now spans part of the River Dee between Cults and Ardoe.

Officially called the St Devenick Bridge, it was built at the expense of the local minister, Dr George Morrison, 150 years ago, so that members of his congregation who lived on the north side of the Dee could cross over from Cults to the kirk at Banchory-Devenick.

The architect of the bridge was John Smith, known as Tudor Johnnie, the first city architect for Aberdeen. However well designed it was in 1840, the passing of a century and a half has seen the paths leading to the bridge, and the bridge itself, steadily erode until only a shadow of its former beauty remains.

Generous as Dr Morrison was in providing the bridge, he left only £50 in his will for its upkeep—a sum which brought in an annual income of £12—nowadays hardly enough to maintain the path to the kirk door, let alone a brig across the Dee!

The good doctor wasn't the only benefactor in the area, however. Another name to be remembered is David Allan, an upholsterer in Aberdeen. Mr Allan had purchased West Cults from the Burnetts of Countesswells, who owned the whole of Cults.

On the occasion of Queen Victoria's Diamond Jubilee in 1897, he gave several acres of his estate to the parish of Peterculter for use as a park. As befits Victorian times, cricket in the summer, and skating in the winter, were much enjoyed. The park, of course, was named after Mr Allan.

Mention of Peterculter recalls that at one time the area was owned by the Durward family, but William the Lion gave the land on the south side of the Dee to the Knights Templar, who protected the pilgrims en route to the Holy Land.

There was already a chapel on the north side dedicated to St Peter, so the Templars built one to St Mary on the south side. Hence there are the two parishes separated by the River Dee. Peterculter is now in the City of Aberdeen District, while Maryculter is in Kincardine and Deeside.

What Dr Morrison sought to unite, nature and man have now rent asunder!

The Shakkin' Briggie—a shadow of its former self.

THE BONNIE CASTLE OF FYVIE TOWERS ABOVE A BITTER CURSE

"Fyvie rigs and Fyvie towers hapless shall thy owners be . . ." so runs the curse placed on Fyvie Castle centuries ago by Thomas the Rhymer.

For, long before the castle was built, there was a priory nearby and like many other church buildings, when it was demolished some of its stones were used for other constructions.

Tradition has it that three special stones were taken from the old priory and taken to the castle—hence the Curse of Fyvie which goes on: "Ye shall hae within yer wa's, fae Holy Kirkland stanes three. One in your highest tower, one in your lady's bower, and ane beneath yer water yett (gate); For these three stanes ye'll never get!"

The existence of one of these stones is known. It is in the Meldrum Tower ("in your highest tower") but there is no trace of the other two stones.

Tradition further claims that the "hapless owners" will never see an heir born within the castle nor will the estate pass in direct line from father to eldest son—as long as "stanes three" remain within the castle.

Despite the curse, Fyvie Castle has existed in one form or another for nearly five and half centuries. Sir Henry Preston had the good luck to capture the son of the Earl of Northumberland, Henry Percy (Hotspur) during the battle of Otterburn in 1388. The ransom was sufficient for him to obtain the lands of Fyvie, the Barony of Formartine and begin the building of the castle.

Each family owning the castle has added a tower bearing the name. Thus over the centuries, five towers have been built—Preston Tower, Meldrum Tower, Seaton Tower, Gordon Tower and finally Leith Tower.

The wheel turned full circle when A J Forbes-Leith became the Laird in 1889. One of the daughters of the founder Sir Henry Preston had married a Forbes all of five centuries before and therefore was an ancestress of the new Laird.

The castle is now in the care of the National Trust for Scotland. If you visit Fyvie, look towards the top of the Preston Tower. There you'll see the figure of a trumpeter.

Legend had it that he is Andrew Lambe in the act of blowing his trumpet towards the Mill of Tifty. At the mill lived his sweetheart—Mill o' Tifty's Annie—but that's another story for another page!

Fyvie Castle—"hapless shall thy owners be . . ."

BRIDGING THE GAPS

Shoppers often lament and sigh about the changing scene in Union Street. But Aberdeen's main street has been undergoing alterations since it was first planned nearly 200 years ago now!

Most people who walk along the street today are unaware that they're literally walking on air—for Union Street is one of the earliest, and probably finest fly-overs in the world.

About half a mile from the Adelphi to Diamond Street is an artificial creation rising between 20 and 50 feet above the normal ground level.

As can be seen from this photograph, taken in 1955, McMillans building has six storeys below street level at the east end of Union Bridge and two storeys above.

It's only when you see such a picture that one realises the tremendous engineering achievement involved in the building of Union Street—a task which sent the city into bankruptcy in 1817!

In 1905, the bridge was widened and the steel spans which can be seen in the photographs were introduced. Other additions were the new parapets designed by Dr William Kelly, whose leopard ornaments were promptly christened Kelly's Cats. The centre of the bridge had bronze panels by Sydney Boyes.

All of this was changed in 1964, when a row of shops was built on the south side of the bridge, eliminating for ever a fine view of Torry, Tullos Hill, and other southerly aspects. Kelly's Cats were removed from the southern parapet and

offers to buy them came from Aberdonians all over the world. You can still see some of the them in the Winter Gardens in the Duthie Park.

Bridge Street, in the left hand corner of the picture, was built between 1865 and 1867, and some of the older readers will remember when tramcars clanked up and down it!

The open space at the side of Bridge Street was occupied by the Palace Buildings, with Pratt and Keith's shop on ground level and the railway's Palace Hotel above. Tragically, the hotel was burned down in October 1941, and demolished some years after the war.

However, C&A's later took over the site and built a store there. But they too have now moved—to the Bon Accord Centre. They're not the only shop or store to have disappeared from the area.

Just to refresh your memory, some of the other shops near the bridge on the south side of Union Street, which existed around the time of the photograph were Style & Mantle; Empress Cafe; Grant's (House Furnishers); Princess Cafe; A C Little; Woolworths; Neave (Hairdresser); Home and Colonial; Boots (Chemists); McMillans; George Pegler; Kennaway; Marshall & Philip; The Picture House; Peter Mitchell (Tobacconist); Paterson, Sons & Marr Wood; A & J Smith (Jewellers); Gordon & Smith (Grocers).

As Omar Khayyam knew . . . *The moving finger writes; and having writ, moves on.*

The Union Bridge has seen many changes.

The author at the well.

UNDER THE HAMMER AT GOLDEN SQUARE

The orginal inhabitants of Golden Square in 1820 would have little difficulty in recognising their former homes and beloved square, apart that is from the rash of motor cars that appear daily, despite the passage of more than a century and a half.

Many Aberdonians and visitors are puzzled by the name Golden Square, and the adjoining streets, North and South Silver Street, Diamond Street, and Ruby Lane. The explanation lies in the fact that the area belonged to the Hammermen, one of the craft guilds of the Seven Incorporated Trades.

The Hammermen, as their name suggests, used hammers for their various trades. Some, such as blacksmiths used big hammers, while small hammers were used by the gold and silversmiths. And it was from the latter group that the area received its precious names!

A happy blend of architectural skills by Aberdeen's leading exponents in the use of granite—Archibald Simpson and "Tudor Johnnie" Smith, the first city architect—led to the creation of this classical Georgian Square. Soon it became one of the most desirable areas of Aberdeen and remains so to the present day.

The original owners would still recognise the cast-iron railings and gates in front of their homes, and in addition the railings which enclosed the grass and trees in the centre (which disappeared during World War II) but have been faithfully restored.

Another wartime casualty was the Hammermen's Well. When these elegant homes were first built they had no individual water supply.

By good fortune, a deep spring was situated on the north side of the square. The water was piped into a rectangular black metal box—the Hammermen's Well.

During the wartime blackout a motor vehicle—a rare visitor to the square in those days—accidentally knocked down the now obsolete well and badly damaged it. It lay, broken and neglected until, at the end of the war in 1945, a good Samaritan rescued it, carefully restored it and re-erected it in his garden at Mannofield.

Some years ago, thanks to the generosity of a well-known Aberdeen businessman, the old well, after 120 years in Golden Square, and 40 years at Mannofield, was returned to the Hammermen. The well is now in the vestibule of Trinity Hall, the home of the Incorporated Trades at the corner of Great Western Road and Holburn Street.

After all these years of public service it must be: "Well done, thou good and faithful servant", for the Hammermen's Well in Golden Square!

WELL, WELL, WELL . . .

At one time in the days before the National Health Service, people had to seek relief for their various ailments wherever they could.

One popular belief was the curative powers of certain waters, particularly that from the Well of Spa in Aberdeen.

For centuries the Spa Well had attracted health-seeking visitors, especially after King James VI's doctor, an Aiberdeen loon, had extolled its virtues.

The well was situated on the bank of the Gilcomston Burn just above the point where it joined the Denburn.

Both these streams—now in culverts underground—frequently burst their banks and fouled the pure mineral water of the Spa.

Another Aiberdeen loon, George Jamesone, born in Schoolhill, was at the Court of James VI's son, Charles I.

In 1635, Jamesone, who felt that the Spa waters had cured him of a stone in the bladder, wrote to the City Magistrates asking their permission to enclose the Spa within a well house.

At the same time this public spirited citizen—because of his "natural affection to this, his native citie, and upon his own chairges"—agreed to also: "mak a playfield for the publict use and benefit of the Town."

So came into being Jameson's Four Neukit Garden alongside the Well of Spa.

The original well-house had on its sandstone gable carvings of a rose, a thistle and a fleur-de-lys, which are, of course, symbols of the Stewart kingdom. Below is the sun—the great life giver.

What cannot be clearly seen in this photograph are the inscriptions. Jamesone's one is above the sun—As Heaven gives me, so I give thee.

Unfortunately, in 1670, some 30 years after Jamesone's death, the well had to be repaired again. This time the benefactor was Baillie Alexander Skene.

His Latin words translated to English, read—May health derived from this spring flow to country and people. The Spa came to life again in 1670.

The last word lies with the town council who had to repair the well once more—so the final inscription at the peak of the well house facade reads in Latin—Anno M DCCC Ll. The work was renewed in the year 1851.

Like many other Aberdeen wells, the Spa has been moved about several times in its long life. About 100 years ago it was moved from its original site across Spa Street to the back of the old infirmary.

Then in 1977 it was moved round the corner to be just outside the Denburn Health Centre.

There is no pure mineral water flowing from the Well of Spa today—nor is it likely to do so in the future. If it did flow once again "to country and people", it would be the same filtered stuff you get from your tap at home.

As the old people used to complain—"This modern water has nae taste nor colour!"

The Well of Spa.

THE DAY THE KINGIE OPENED OOR BRIGGIE!

While the old Bridge of Dee is more than 450 years old, the new Bridge of Dee—otherwise the King George VI Bridge—is just past its 50th birthday.

Built to take the strain of increasing motor traffic off the Auld Brig, it was intended to be the main arterial route into the city from the south.

King George VI opened the bridge on March 10, 1941. He was accompanied by the Lord Provost of the time, Tommy (later Sir Thomas) Mitchell. Tommy never liked making prepared speeches and, because the day was a windy one, he had difficulty in reading his notes. Suddenly he burst out, "Och I've lost my place. Never min', Kingie, jist open yer briggie!".

Provost from 1938 until 1947, he was knighted in 1943 and remained a great favourite with the Royal Family.

When the bridge was designed, before the outbreak of war in 1939, it was planned to have four sculpted granite lions at each corner. For various reasons, the plan was abandoned. The granite slabs lay about for 30 years until three of them were put up at Hazlehead Park and given the title Hazlehenge. The fourth block of granite is to be seen in the Centre of Bon-Accord Square as a memorial to the famous Aberdeen architect, Archibald Simpson.

A model of one of the lions, half its original size, could be seen in the Duthie Park's Winter Gardens. Curiously enough, in the same area is the Mount Cottage Fountain which at one time stood at 45 Mount Street, once occupied by Sir Thomas Mitchell.

Upstream from the new Bridge of Dee is the original crossing of the river, before any bridges existed. This is the Foords of Dee, just about opposite the former Ruthrieston Junior Secondary School.

The low level of the water at this point allowed travellers from the south to cross comparatively safely, at least in the summer, and still tempts fishermen there to this very day.

Most river crossings were safeguarded by a medieval stronghold and the Foords were no exception. Ruadri the Mormaer—or Earl of Mar—and his wife Muredach, had their castle there. Thus the town or village which grew up around it was named after them—Ruadri's town . . . or, as it is known today, Ruthrieston.

George VI Bridge . . . past its 50th birthday.

KIRK WITHOUT A ROOF

Apart from the man-made structures, this scene has remained practically unchanged in the course of several million years. The River Dee had its outlet to the sea at the Bay of Nigg before the Ice Age changed the course of the river to its present channel.

The ruins of St Fittick's Kirk in the foreground also have a long history. Legend has it that St Fittick—an Irish disciple of St Ninian—was shipwrecked and came ashore at this point. Six centuries later in 1242, a church was built on the site. It is said that Irish soil, blessed by St Patrick, was sprinkled on the ground accordingly, no worms or snakes are ever to be found in the area!

August 30th is St Fittick's Day, and it is then that, traditionally, the local people made their visit to the Saint's well—now washed away by the sea—to drink the water, famed for its healing powers.

For 300 years the church was Catholic. Following the Reformation, it became Episcopalian, and it remained so until 1716 when the minister, Richard Maitland was deposed for praying for James VIII (the Old Pretender), instead of King George!

The belfry still carries Mr Maitland's initials but the bell itself was removed to the new kirk upon Nigg Brae in 1829, when St Fittick's was abandoned.

The bell was made in 1759 by John Mowatt, blacksmith of Old Aberdeen. It has a legend on it—"Sabata Pango, Funra Plango"—Sabbaths I proclaim, at funerals I toll.

Beside the door were a few rusted links of chain—all that remains of the "jougs" in which rumour-mongers, minor offenders and "scolds"—women who nagged their husbands—were fastened to do penance in sight of the worshippers as they passed into the kirk.

But not everyone was allowed into the building. There were lepers in the Tullos valley as elsewhere in Aberdeen. Not allowed to mingle with the other worshippers, they had to stand outside and look through a little oblong opening (The Leper's Squint) in the wall. There, within sight and sound of the priest but unseen by the congregation, the unfortunate sufferers could join in the service.

The graveyard contains many old tombstones. At the east end lies the grave of 42 men from a crew of 44 of the whaler "Oscar" which sank in Greyhope Bay on April 1, 1813, and whose name is commemorated in Oscar Road, Torry.

Nowadays the auld kirk stands roofless, the bell no longer rouses the congregations from Downies, Burnbanks, Cove, Tullos hill and hollow, and in the graveyard—"Each in his narrow cell for ever laid: The rude forefathers of the hamlet sleep."

The ruins of St Fittick's Kirk.

NOT FOR UNDER-16s!

During one of my weekly Friday perambulations around the Castlegate Market, I exchanged some pleasantries with a country chiel fae Foggieloan. He spoke nostalgically about the auld days of when he'd been fee'd as a halflin and how he still kept two pairs of his Granda's Nicky Tams!

Bursting into rhyme, if not song, he quoted:

First I got on for Baillie loon,
Syne I got on for third,
And syne of course I hid to get
The Horseman's grippin' Word.

And then queried if I knew anything about The Word?

It so happened that 50 years ago, my stepfather, who came from deepest Buchan, had told me about the Horseman's Society. Normally The Word was not given to a loon under the age of 16 but this injunction was apparently sometimes broken.

This photograph, taken just before the outbreak of war in 1939, may seem to show a way of life that has existed since time immemorial, but really only came into being 200 years ago, thanks to a Scotsman, John Small of Dalkeith.

He invented the iron swing plough needing only two horses, which in time displaced the old style wooden plough which required up to 12 oxen to drag it (called in the dialect: "a twal owsen ploo"). A whole band of men were recruited to keep the ploo going—one held the handles, another walked backwards to watch the cattle, a third went ahead with a mallet to break up lumps of soil, the fourth, the "gadman" had a long pole to goad the lumbering beasts.

All this effort by man and beast scratched about half an acre a day. As a local critic observed—"more fit to raise laughter than raise soil".

The replacement of oxen by horses gave to young farm workers the necessity of having handling skills that would enable them to move up the ladder of promotion in the ranks of the horsemen. For the hierarchy which existed was as rigid as any army in their lines of command.

At the top was the grieve (usually an ex-horseman) who was in charge of all the outworkers. Then came the foreman, who was the senior ploughman. Next, depending on the number of pairs of horses, came the second, third, or even fourth horseman. Some halflins (boy or half loons) might later choose to be coo baillies—in charge of cattle, while others worked as orramen (who could turn their hand to any job on the farm).

But the horsemen always outranked all others in status, hence most young men longed to be a brother in the Horseman's Society.

The first approach to a young hopeful would be an envelope addressed to him, containing a single horse hair! After he had puzzled over this cryptic message for a while he would then receive a second message to come to a meeting at midnight, usually "thru the c'aff hoose door" (Chaffhouse—part of the threshing mill).

The climax of the ceremony came when the initiate, after handing over a bottle of whisky, some oatcakes, and cheese, took the oath and shook hands with Auld Nick—a stirk's foot painted with luminous paint to make it glow in the dark.

My stepfather when shaking hands with the Deil was struck across the back of the hand with a trace-chain, a mark he carried all his life, but he had the secret of The Word—which, in theory, could control two sets of unruly craiturs—horses and women!

Members of the society were alleged to be able to "reist a horse" (make it stop and no other man could move it) or make it move for him only along with other uncanny powers.

And the Horseman's grippin' Word? Well, as I said at the beginning—it wasn't for a loon under 16—I never did find out!

A mythical horse from a Pictish stone.

A country scene for the past 200 years.

THE LEGACY OF MALCOLM'S CROSSED SWORDS

The Highland Games season like many other traditional activities, is not what it used to be, for at one time most, if not every, small town and village had its own games or a gathering.

Both world wars led to a temporary stopping of the annual Highland events, many never to re-start. And various taxes, especially VAT, meant that the hard-working committees which organised the games—usually on a voluntary basis—found it all too much and simply gave up.

Nevertheless, all is not gloom. Highland Games are first class attractions, especially when the weather is good. In Aberdeen there have been some sort of games for over 150 years . . . the Bon-Accord Highland Gathering, the Aberdeen Police Games and the Highland Association Games. Aberdeen Highland Games, held during the Bon Accord Festival week, attracts a crowd of around 15,000.

So, despite setbacks, old traditions die hard. Some historians claim that Highland Games go back as far as King Malcolm Canmore, 900 years ago! He held games in order to choose the strongest men for his bodyguard and the swiftest runners for messengers.

To many people, the most picturesque part of the event is the dancing. The picture illustrates the correct style.

Note the way his fingers are poised for the Highland Fling. This is said to be a pre-hunting dance, in which the dancers imitate the deer's antlers with their arms and fingers, while the feet represent the deer's hooves pawing the hillside.

Probably the oldest dance seen nowadays is the Ghillie Calum or sword dance. Again, Malcolm Canmore is given the credit for originating this dance, when he placed a defeated opponent's sword below his and danced in triumph over them.

Sean Trews—or old trousers—dates from the Diskilting Act, following Culloden, when it was forbidden to wear the kilt, and the dance shows the difficulty that a Highlander had in adjusting to the unfamiliar troosers!

From our own area comes the Reel of Tulloch, said to have originated in the village of Tulloch near Ballater. The story goes that the church congregation grew weary of waiting for the minister to appear one frosty Sunday morning.

To keep the cold at bay they drank the communion wine and began stamping their feet and clapping their hands to keep the circulation going—thus was born the Reel of Tulloch!

The unco-guid will be delighted to know that all the participants were refused communion and not one lived out the rest of the year!

The swirl o' the kilt.

ROBIN WAS A ROVIN' LAD

On January 25, Robert Burns was born in the year 1759.
> *"Our Monarch's hindmaist year but ane,*
> *Was Five and twenty days begun;*
> *Twas then a blast of Janwar*
> *Win' Blew hansel in on Robin,"*

Toasts to Scotland's national poet will be given as warmly in America as in Russia and from Land's End to John o' Groats. And we in the North-east should be rightly proud of his strong links with this area.

For although most Scots people would agree that Burns lived near "Auld Ayr, whom ne'er a town surpasses", how many know that the "auld clay biggin" he was born in was built by his father William Burnes, who came from the farm of Brawlinmuir near Drumlithie, south of Stonehaven.

The Burnes family had lived in that area since the time of Robert the Bruce over 600 years ago. The poet's father had been forced to leave Drumlithie because of the part the Burneses had taken in supporting the Old Pretender, James Stewart, father of Bonnie Prince Charlie in 1715.

The Burnes family had followed their landowner George Keith the Earl of Marischal of Scotland, and Laird of Dunottar Castle into the Jacobite army. The Earl was ruined after the failure of the 1715 Rising and had to sell off his land.

Eventually, the Burnes family also left the area and moved south in the 1740s.

Robert Burns remembered all this when he showed his opinion of the Hanoverian "German Lairdie" by scratching on a window pane in Stirling Castle:
> *"The injured Stewart race is gone.*
> *A race outlandish fills their throne:*
> *An idiot race, to honour lost—*
> *Who knows them best, despise them most!"*

As a young man Robert called himself Burnes but later changed to the south-western Scottish pronunciation of Burns. A similar example is the North-eastern name of Forbes—pronounced Forbess locally but changed further south.

In 1786, in search of new material, and wishing to see his surviving family relatives, Burns made a tour of the North-east. He certainly visited the city of Aberdeen, which he described as a lazy town!

During his stay of one night, he met James Chalmers at the New Inn. Chalmers was the printer of the Aberdeen Journal—a forerunner of the present Evening Express and Press and Journal.

Later, Robert called at Laurencekirk and stayed at the Gardenstoun Arms Hotel where a plaque on the wall commemorates his visit. Whether he visited Glenbervie churchyard, Drumlithie, is not recorded. For that is where his ancestors—and incidentally mine, the Balfours—lie buried side by side.

In a few years time, we'll be thinking about the 200th anniversary!
> *"He'll hae misfortunes great and sma',*
> *But aye a heart a boon them a',*
> *He'll be a credit till us a'—*
> *We'll a' be proud o' Robin."*

". . . a boon them a,"

SUNSET SONGS

History can sometimes be discovered at two levels—the official version written in textbooks, often with unacceptable details omitted—or at a different level, folklore, which is the unwritten experience of the people at the receiving end of things. Often this tradition is transmitted in a dialect unknown to outsiders and is usually in verse or song.

A collection of such unique folksongs was made by Gavin Greig, a Buchan dominie (or schoolteacher) who, along with the Reverend James Duncan, gathered a vast number of the local oral traditions.

These songs are often referred to nowadays as Bothy Ballads, under the misapprehension that they were only performed in bothies which is where most northern unmarried male farmworkers were housed.

However, in the area where the songs mainly originated—Aberdeenshire, Banffshire, and in the Howe o' the Mearns—there were few bothies; the men living in the chaumers, often over the stable, and eating in the farm kitchen.

It was in Moray, Nairn and in the south of Kincardine that the bothy system operated—a one-roomed building where the single men slept, and also cooked the foodstuffs allowed them by the farmer instead of board. So these last areas had many bothies but few ballads!

The drawing shows just such a farm worker sitting on a corn-kist and supping oot a' a brose caup—wooden bowls—many of them made in Aberdeen at Cuparstone (the hamlet of the wooden cup-makers) and sold at the Timmer Market.

Most of these single men had been feed at one of the local fairs—Aikey Brae, Lowrin Fair, or at the big markets like Muckle Friday in Aberdeen and Porter Fair in Turriff. The farmers who took them on liked to have a good reputation in order to engage suitable men. What they feared was a bad name and this was spread around by the North-east's own bush telegraph—the folksong.

The men would, after work, sit on the corn-kists and, drumming in time with their heels, sing corn-kisters—warning their fellows of various greedy farmers, the bad food, and the poor working conditions:

> Come all you jolly ploughboys,
> I pray you have a care,
> Beware o' going to Swaggers,
> For he'll be in Porter Fair.

The farmer's wife, responsible for feeding the men of the chaumer, was also the target for criticism:

> The breid was thick, the brose was thin,
> The broth they were like bree:
> I chased the barley rounn' the plate
> An' a' I got was three!

Both men are wearing nicky tams, or wull tams, leather straps to take the weight of their wet trouser bottoms off their galluses (or braces). These days were never forgotten, wherever they went:

> Fitiver it's my lot to be,
> The bobbies or the trams,
> I'll niver forget the happy days
> I wore my nicky tams!

Cornkist chiels suppin' their brose.

17

THERE'S A COACH COMIN' IN

Rob Roy, William Wallace, Robert Burns, The Earl of Aberdeen, The Duke of Gordon and the Earl of Erroll—sounds like a roll-call of famous Scottish names—but in fact are the titles of stagecoaches of a past era.

As late as 1865 there was still a regular stagecoach service to Ellon. The journey took about two hours, compared to today's 20 minutes by car.

Travel more than a century ago was most uncomfortable! The seats inside the coach were unsprung and stuffed with horsehair. Generally, there were six people cramped within and if you couldn't afford such a luxury, then there were bare boards for 12 other passengers up on the roof, alongside the luggage!

Royal Mail coaches were especially colourful, with their livery of maroon and black, and the Royal Coat of Arms displayed in gold. The driver wore a uniform, as did the guard, who carried a pair of flintlock pistols and blunderbuss!

If you had business in London, it took 69 hours to get there! Horses had to be changed about every 15 miles, so there were some 36 changes between Aberdeen and the capital.

In addition, there were stops for meals and liquid refreshments, as well as bed and breakfast. Obviously, only the very well-to-do could afford to travel such long distances! Local journeys were only a little better. Peterhead had a regular service which left Aberdeen at 3pm in the afternoon and arrived in the Blue Toon at 8pm, some five hours later. The route was through Balmedie, Ellon, Toll of Birness, and Cruden Bay.

There are still memories of those days in hotels with names like The Coach and Horses and The Post House. The busiest staging-post on the road to Peterhead was probably the New Inn at Ellon, which was a half-way house.

In the city itself, travel for short distances was by sedan-chair, usually carried by the stalwarts of the Aberdeen Shore Porters. The last recorded use of such transport was just over a century ago, when Lord Provost Sir Alexander Anderson, at the age of 85, attended his wife's funeral, carried in a sedan-chair.

Ironically, the main road through Aberdeen is named after the Provost—Anderson Drive. And about the same time as he was being carried through the streets of the city, two Germans from Cologne—Doctor Otto and Herr Daimler were developing a petrol engine which was to be the motive power for the motor car!

Thus within a lifetime, we have literally gone from two-man sedan chairs to two-car families!

Has the wheel turned full circle?

How they travelled in style in the good old days!. The horse-drawn carriage passes a long line of motor cars.

A sedan chair. Carried by the stalwarts of the Shore Porters Society and probably last used at the funeral of Lord Provost Anderson's wife, just over a century ago.

Gargoyle? Poet? Ironmonger?

20

FROM RAGG'S TO . . . COPPERS!

Most visitors to Provost Skene's House in the Guestrow pass without an upward glance at a grimacing, bearded face looking down at them from eyeless sockets, on the south-east corner of the building.

Older readers may recall when the fearsome head was to be found on the wall of No. 35 Broad Street at the corner of Ragg's Lane. The lane ran from Broad Street to the Guestrow and was named after Baillie Alexander Ragg, a Magistrate of the City, who bought the land in 1702. The worthy Baillie died in 1719 and was buried in what is now the path in front of the door to the West Church of St Nicholas. Centuries of footsteps have obliterated any inscription on his tombstone and even his other memorial, in the shape of the lane called after him, disappeared in 1959 when St Nicholas House began to be built.

Those who notice the grim, snarling visage always ask— why is it there? Well, you can take your choice! Firstly, it was put on the wall of No. 35 by Ragg himself, who was on the Council when the Mannie Well was first placed in the Castlegate in 1708. A comparison of the faces at the corners of the well-roof show a resemblance to that of the one under discussion, which is also similar to those found at the mouth of the old city wells.

Second version: the shop at No. 35 was occupied at one time by a bookseller, who obtained the head, which is that of the bearded, blind, Greek poet, Homer, to advertise his stock of classical books.

Or lastly, and this is the story which most Aberdonians love to hear, is that the face was created by George Russel, a sculptor, then living at No. 35, who had a grudge against a neighbouring ironmonger—Alexander Stephen—and to spite him, modelled a likeness of the tradesman, showing his most irate, unhappy face. The caricature was then put in a prominent position designed to infuriate Stephen every time he passed Ragg's Lane!

Russel may have harboured a dislike of ironmongers but he had a warm spot for police constables and the scaffies who swept the streets. On his death in 1898 he left some money in trust (a tiny amount nowadays) to be given yearly to each constable and scavanger. But, obviously still nursing some long-past grievance, he made a proviso that no promoted officer of the Force, nor foreman of cleansing, was to receive any monies whatsoever!

Thus nearly a century after his death, George Russel's grudge still remains in the public eye, while his generosity jingles in the policemen's pockets!

CA' CANNY WAKKIN ON THE BRIG O' BALGOWNIE!

A recent news item that Aberdeen District Council has decided the path leading from the Brig o' Balgownie to Balgownie Road in the Bridge of Don area is to be resurfaced, is the continuation of a 700 years' involvement between the Brig and Aberdeen City.

And the fact that the City Fathers are to ask Grampian Regional Council for a grant to carry out the work is also an auld sang to a well-known tune!

For much of the history of the bridge is the story of its repairs and how silver for it was obtained from the civic pooch.

Tradition has it that the Brig was started as early as 1290 in order to make a road "to this toun out of Buchan, Gareauch, and ither pairts thairaboot".

However, it was not until around 1320 that the work was completed. Thanks for its construction is usually given to King Robert the Bruce, but the money really came from Bishop Henry Cheyne, whom Bruce had banished from his See at the nearby St Machar's Cathedral.

The Bishop was later restored to his position and his accumulated revenues were ordered to be spent on the bridge.

When the Reformation came to Scotland in 1560, the silver and brass work, capes and ornaments from the "Parroche Kirk" were "roupit" to pay for on-going repairs to the Brig. In 1604, it was the old, old story—"the Brig is decaying and becum ruynous . . . and will faill in schort space alluterlie."

It so happened that the "haill toun, Burgesses, craftsmen and inhabitants" had raised £500 to help the good Protestant people of Geneva, who were being persecuted by the Catholic Duke of Savoy.

Built with a Bishop's purse and doomed by a Devil's curse!

The council coolly decided that "praisit be to God, the same towne of Geneva hes nocht a present necessitit thairof" and therefore the money was spent on the bridge!

A solution to the perennial problem of repairing the Brig came the following year, 1605, when Sir Alexander Hay of Whitburgh left the modest sum of £2.5s 8½d (£2.28) for the upkeep of the bridge.

This money was wisely invested and when the new Bridge of Don was built further downstream in 1830, the cost was £16,000, which came from interest on Sir Alexander's timely gift.

Thomas The Rhymer (of Ercildoune) who made so many gloomy prophecies about buildings and people in Scotland did not omit to mention the Brig o' Balgownie:

> *Brig o' Balgownie, wicht's thy wa',*
> *Wi a wife's ae son, an a mare's ae foal,*
> *Doon shalt thou fa'.*

Lord George Byron, who was educated at Aberdeen Grammar School, and "a wife's ae son" was terrified as he rode over the bridge in case his horse was a "a mare's ae foal", an incident which he could recall to the end of his days, and was included in one of his epic poems.

Thus between Henry Cheyne's contribution to the bridge building and "True" Thomas's woeful forecast as to its fate, there arose another couplet.

> *Built by a Bishop's purse*
> *And doomed by the Devil's curse.*

However, after 700 years of use the Brig still stands—but only for foot passengers—ye darna be ower canny!

The Black-Nook alehouse stood at the far side of the Brig.

WISHING THE OLD WELLS WELL

Aberdeen District Council's decision to spend over £1000 on the restoration of the Gibberie Wallie shows a wise appreciation of the citizens' affection for ancient landmarks.

The Firhill Well is the proper name of the Gibberie Wallie, and older readers might remember when it stood in Firhill Place, off the Spital, almost opposite Orchard Street. That was in 1937.

The well, which dates from about 1721, was removed from its original site and placed beside the Sunnybank bowling green. And its nickname? It came from the days—long gone—when Gibberie-wifies sold gingerbread and "ither sich smachrie", while seated on the stone benches beside the well.

Most areas had their local well. The district of Gilcomston had one on the croft belonging to the Knights of the Hospital of St John of Jerusalem. Just over a century ago, when Rosemount Viaduct was built, the well was removed and placed under the flight of granite steps which leads from Skene Street down to Upper Denburn.

St John's Well was again moved, in 1955—this time to Albyn Place—outside No. 21, which is the Venerable Order of St John's Nursing Home, thus retaining a historical link with its original benefactors.

Another well which was disturbed during the building of Rosemount Viaduct and Union Terrace was the Corbie Well. It used to stand at the side of the Denburn until the burn was piped under the railway line. The well was then removed to Union Terrace Gardens (the Trainie Parkie). Above the well was part of the weathercock from the steeple of old St Nicholas Church (the Mither Kirk), which was burned down in 1874. It was supported by one of the central lamp-posts from the Bow Brig, which crossed the Denburn at the foot of Windmill Brae.

When the Brig was demolished to make way for the railway line, it was built into one of the arches under Union Terrace, and can still be seen just below Robert Burns' statue.

There was also a fragment from one of the bells of the kirk, named Auld Lowrie—short for St Lawrence. This great bell was gifted to the church by Provost William Leith of Ruthrieston in 1351, after he had accidentally slain one of the city baillies.

I know that we sometimes have great arguments in the council chambers but nothing as drastic as that! After all—all's well that ends well!

The Firhill Well or Gibberie Wallie.

THE SLINGS AND ARROWS OF OUTRAGEOUS FORTUNE

Did famous film producer Franco Zefferelli meet more ghosts than Hamlet's father, when he filmed his new version of the Prince of Denmark in one of the North-east's most atmospheric castles?

Just south of Stonehaven, Dunnottar is on a spectacular site—a headland rising 150 feet straight out of the sea, which surrounds it on three sides. It must have plenty of ghosts, dating as it does from the days of the Picts, who had a fort there.

Donald, King of Alba, died there fighting the Danish raiders who landed on the coast—perhaps killed by one of Hamlet's forebears?

But the name most associated with Dunnottar Castle is that of Keith. The family were the Earl Marischals of Scotland. Sir William Keith decided to settle in the Mearns about the end of the 14th century, following his marriage to Margaret, the daughter of the Thane of Cowie. Ironically, Shakespeare's other great tragic figure, Macbeth, was the Thane of Cawdor.

Thus began a 300 year period during which the Keiths built more and more additions to their stronghold at Dunnottar. Eventually, it became one of the largest castles in Scotland.

On the one site there is a range of buildings dating from the days of bows and arrows to fairly modern artillery.

For Dunnottar is "one of the ruins that Cromwell knocked about a bit". He was determined to obtain the Crown Jewels of Scotland which had been placed there for safekeeping by Charles II—the so-called Merry Monarch. The castle surrendered after a bombardment from Cromwell's guns, placed near the present-day War Memorial on Black Hill.

But the jewels and the Honours of Scotland were not there, having been hidden in the church at Kinneff, some miles down the coast.

When Keith got his castle back it was in a sorry state. But in 1718 even worse was to come. The 10th Earl Marishal was convicted of treason for supporting the Old Pretender and had to flee Scotland. The castle fell into the ruinous state it is today.

Nevertheless, Hamlet, in the earthly shape of actor Mel Gibson, brought the castle to life again until the final: "Goodnight, sweet Prince, and flights of angels sing thee to thy rest!"

Then Dunnottar's ghosts went to sleep again for another few centuries.

The spectacular Dunnottar Castle, a Keith stronghold for centuries.

TALES O' THE PLAID AND PIPES

Probably the most photographed event at any Highland Games will be the march of the massed pipe bands.

A Pipe Major, as pictured here, is thought to be representative of The Flower of Scotland. Yet at one time, following the Battle of Culloden, it was forbidden to wear the Highland dress—or even tartan—in any form whatsoever.

In November 1746, James Reid, a piper in Bonnie Prince Charlie's Jacobite army, was hanged because, in the eyes of the law, the bagpipes were an instrument of war!

However, 50 years after the end of the Jacobite Risings, the wars with France saw the government realise the need for Scottish fighting men. Soon such regiments as the Seaforth Highlanders, the Argyll and Sutherland Highlanders and, of course the Gordon Highlanders, appeared.

In many British Army regiments, the bugle is used to inform the soldiers what to do. But in a Highland Regiment, most of the commands are played on the pipes. In the morning, reveille is the pipe-tune Hey Johnnie Cope, are ye wauken' yet? Marching is to tunes such as Cock o' The North, and Lights Out at the end of the day is signalled by Lie doon sodjer laddie on yer wee puckle straw.

There are popular myths that the great Highland bagpipe was being played by the Picts when they attacked the Romans, and that a Greek writer recorded the Highlanders as playing them in the first century AD.

Well, the pipes are old. The Chinese had them, as did the Persians, and Chaucer mentions them in his Canterbury Tales of 600 years ago. But the bagpipes as we recognise them today, with three drones, came into being only about 300 years ago.

At one time, most towns and cities had their official piper who would play through the streets to waken the citizens for their day's work and play again in the evening. The piper had to go round at 4am—or lose his wages and be imprisoned for eight days!

The evening round would be about six o' clock—no factory whistles in those days!

In Aberdeen, we had a town piper from about 1507 to 1603, when it was decided to dispense with his services. Not because of cost but because of culture—in the words of the Town Records "the piper is dischargit frae his duties as it is an uncivil form to be usit in sic a famous burgh and he is often found fault with by strangers."

In Perth, however, the death of the town piper was much regretted ". . . the music having an inexpressibly soothing and delightful effect in the morning". Perhaps the listener's reaction depended on the distance away from the piper!

The bagpipes have led the Scots into battle, and into a merry dance on social occasions. Next time you hear them, reflect on the effect they've had on Scots throughout the centuries, for the sound of the great Highland bagpipe is the sound of Scotland.

Cock o' the North.

FRIARS, FLUX AND FLAX

Aberdeen can claim, like Rome, to be built on seven hills. Castlehill, St Katherine's Hill—which stood between the Shiprow and Union Street—and the Heading Hill (behind Castlehill) are some.

The Broad Hill was part of a number of hills demolished to make way for the City Hospital—known in my youth as Cunnigar (Rabbity) Hill. The Gallow Hill near Erroll Street and the Trinity Cemetry, as the name suggests, was the site of the gallows until 1776.

Porthill (from the French word for gate—porte) is at the top of the Gallowgate (road to the gallows—gata being the Scandinavian for a road). And finally, as seen in this photograph—Woolmanhill (the hill of the wool man).

In 1222, Alexander II emulated the gift of his predecessor, William the Lion, who had granted property to the Red Friars, by giving land in the Woolmanhill area to the Dominican or Black Friars. The street of the same name commemorates the king's generosity.

During the 15th century on the site of the Old Infirmary buildings, at a point where the public could look up at them, were held religious or miracle plays. A great favourite in Aberdeen was the one called Holy Blude.

The cast was mainly drawn from the craftsmen of the city. The smiths and the hammermen were the three Kings of Cologne, while the tailors dressed up as Our Lady, St Bride, and St Helen! Angels and Bishops were played by the hide merchants, or skinners.

Unfortunately, familiarity with saintly personages didn't polish up the manners or conduct of the tradesmen, because a great dispute arose as to which trade should play which part.

The Town Council was called in to arbitrate—and the skinners were ordered to be the tormentors of St Stephen—a suitable role? St George was now to be a member of the bonnet makers.

Whereas the monks had at one time looked after the sick in their monastic hospitals, it was fitting that the Town Council chose Woolmanhill to build an infirmary in the 1740's.

Over the years, continued extensions had to be made until a century later it was decided to build an entirely new hospital. This classic example of architecture can still be seen dominating Woolmanhill. It is the work of Archibald Simpson.

Later parts were added by father and son, William and John Smith. Even so, by 1936, Aberdeen Royal Infirmary had to move to Foresterhill to even larger premises.

Just behind the Old Infirmary is the "dark satanic mills" of Mr John Maberly who in 1811 introduced linen manufacture to the Broadford Works.

The red-brick castellated factory is now a listed building and is under discussion as to its future.

At one time in this area stood the Woolmanhill Drill Hall, home of the Gordon Highlanders (TA) for many years. It has now totally disappeared, which only goes to show that "old soldiers never die—they only fade away!"

Woolmanhill . . . built on one of Aberdeen's seven hills.

TRAILING FOR SCOTLAND'S FISH

Among the attractions for visitors to Scotland is a Fishing Heritage Trail. The trail follows the line of the east and North-east coast, for at one time there were said to be about 70 villages in the 150 mile stretch from the Banffshire coast to Montrose, mainly dependant on fishing for a livelihood.

Many of them had no harbour, except those in the Peterhead, Fraserburgh, Aberdeen and Montrose areas, and depended on a sandy beach or break in the cliffs to pull their small open boats beyond the reach of the tide. It was probably the greatest collective in Scotland of people devoted entirely to fishing.

Fishing has gone on in this area for over a thousand years. Bronze hooks dating from the time of the Romans have been found in the Foords o' Dee near the Auld Brig. And it was this type of fishing, on two miles of line and with 2000 hooks, which enabled the North-east fisherman to catch his prey— cod, ling, skate, halibut or haddock.

The fishermen would be in sma bates or muckle bates— small or big boats—and would venture out up to 60 miles from port, remaining out for four or five days. Their wives also shared in the toil, collecting mussels for bait, putting the bait on the hooks, helping haul the boats in and out of the water and carrying their husbands on their backs through the surf, so that he could be dryshod. A fishwife would have agreed with the old adage, a woman's work is never done!

Just over a century ago, in order to reach more distant fishing grounds, decked or half-decked sailing boats were introduced, for the catch was no longer to be white fish but the herring or Silver Darlings caught by nets. The new type of boats were the Baldie (called after Garibaldi, the great Italian patriot), the Fifie (from Fife), the Scaffie (skiff) and the Zulu (the Zulu war took place in 1879).

The season began on the north-west coast in the early summer and followed the shoals of herring around the north and east until they reached the English ports of Yarmouth and Lowestoft. Along with the fleet went the teams of fish quines who cleaned and salted the herrings before packing them in barrels for export to Russia, Germany and north-east Europe in general.

Further change came at the turn of the century when sail gave way to steam power. From 38 trawlers operating from Aberdeen 100 years ago, by 1914 there were 249.

Older readers will remember the Smokey Joes with their sail set as they went down the Navigation Channel, as seen in this photograph.

Of course it's all changed now. In fact, we're practically back to the days when there was no large-scale fishing from North-east Scotland. For many reasons the bulk of the fishing fleet has steadily dwindled. After many centuries we can no longer claim—wir ain fish guts for wir ain sea-maws.

A Smokey Joe sets off in its search for the Silver Darlings.

"From the fury of the Vikings, Good Lord deliver us?"

A NORSE SAGA

Nowadays, the people of the North-east of Scotland welcome many overseas visitors, who usually arrive here in the summer. But 900 years ago, one particular group was certainly most unwelcome—they were the so-called Summer Wanderers—Vikings who used to go on raiding trips during the summer months. The Vikings were Scandinavians from Norway, Sweden and Denmark. As they came from the north they were called Northmen or Norsemen. This became corrupted into Normans and when some settled in the northern part of France, the area became Normandy.

The sea warriors didn't ignore Scotland in their travels. By 1034 King Duncan could claim to rule the Britons of Strathclyde, the Angles of Lothian, the Scots of Argyll and the Picts north of the Forth, but he had to accept that the islands to the north—Orkney and Shetland—and to the west—the Hebrides—as well as Caithness and Sutherland (the southern lands) were firmly in the grip of the Vikings!

On summer raids the Norsemen were led by their king's son, Eric Bloodaxe. Other raiders had equally colourful names—Lief the Lucky, Magnus Bluetooth, Harald Fairhair, Helgi the Lean. Names were given according to reputation in battle: Thorfinn, Skullsplitter and Eric Brainbiter, or by appearance: Magnus Barelegs, Ragnor Hairybreeks or even Onund Woodenleg!

Buchan was a favourite target for summer raids, but one year the Vikings got more than they had bargained for. At Gamrie they were defeated and the skulls of three of their leaders were built into the walls of the old church there. It is said that the skulls were still visible just over a century ago, but today they have disappeared.

In 1014, a large force of Danes, led by Prince Canute landed at Cruden Bay and built a small fort on the present-day golf course.

The Scots—led by King Malcolm—were again too good for them, capturing the Danish camp and killing the leaders. The King of Denmark sent over a slab of blue marble to mark the Danish grave. This stone could be seen for many centuries, beside the east gate of Cruden Parish Church. There was also a chapel built on the battle site, and a well to this day bears its name—St Olaf—probably one of the few Norse names in the district.

For, unlike the situation in the northern and western isles and on the mainland to the north, there was never a permanent Viking settlement in the North-east area. In fact, Aberdeen became the Scottish base for attempts to re-conquer Caithness and Sutherland. But even then the city itself (Aberdion) became the target for Viking attacks.
An old Norse Saga, or story, tells how:

> *"I heard the overthrow of the people,*
> *The clash of broken arms was loud,*
> *The King destroyed the peace,*
> *Of dwellers in Aberdion."*

So, when you say your prayers tonight, thank God that you don't have to give the ancient prayer of the monks—"From the fury of the Vikings, Good Lord deliver us!"

A SAINTLY DAY FOR SANTA AND ABERDEEN

December 6 passes totally unheeded by most Aberdonians who probably have more important things like Christmas shopping to think about. But December 6 has a link between both Aberdonians and Christmas, it's the feast-day of Saint Nicholas, the Patron Saint of Aberdeen.

For over the centuries the Saint's name has become corrupted into Santa Niclaus and finally to Santa Claus! The Mither Kirk of the city was named after him—St Nicholas Church—and has been in existence for at least 800 years. The earliest stonework is two hundred years older than St Machar's in The Aulton.

"St Nicholas' stately structure here doth stand,
No paroch Church can match't in all the land."

Nicholas was a Bishop in the 4th Century A.D. and his good works included the giving of dowries to impoverished maidens to help them get suitable husbands.

Probably his most famous act happened when he was passing by a tavern. Nicholas heard the screaming of children and discovered that the inn-keeper, being short of meat, had put three children in a pot of boiling water to make a meal for unsuspecting guests!

The Saint restored the victims to life and it is this scene which is on the reverse of the City's Common seal. The other side of the seal has the coat of arms which most people recognise.

This is the three towers with a double line around them and two leopards supporting the shield, with above them the motto Bon Accord.

Before the coming of Grampian Region in the mid 1970s, this was the badge that used to be on the sides of the trams and buses and on the policemen's hats. It is still worn around the Lord Provost's neck as well as being on the "scaffies barras", and behind the Presiding Justice in the District Court.

The double line—or tressure—is a rare mark of royal favour and was only granted to one other city in Scotland—Perth. The leopards are also a special royal grant—probably from William the Lion.

On the shield are the colours of Santa Claus—red and white. This is why Aberdeen Football Club—the Dons—wear these colours.

Of course older readers will remember when the Dons wore black and gold stripes and were nicknamed the Wasps but that was some 50-odd years ago!

Saint Nicholas, in the days before the Russian Revolution, was the patron saint of Imperial Russia. In addition, Nicholas is the Patron Saint of Merchants and Traders as well as Pawnbrokers and Robbers. I suppose Aberdeen has had its share of all of them at one time!

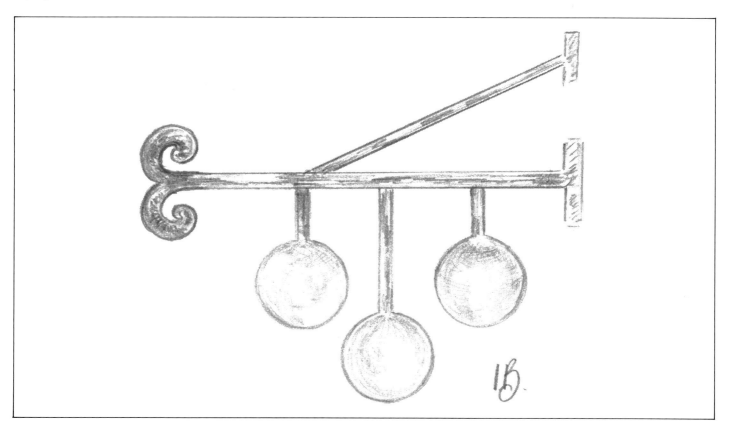

The Pawnbrokers' sign—Saint Nicholas was also their patron saint!

A BRIG O'ER TROUBLED TIMES

The Auld Brig, the Bridge of Dee is once again, the scene of a running skirmish, as it has been a number of times over the centuries.

This time, however, it's a war of words and not the Marquis of Montrose battling his way into the town, as he did in 1639.

The current debate is whether the Bridge of Dee should be again widened, as it was 1841, to accommodate modern traffic, or whether a new bridge should be built further upstream.

When it was completed in 1527, the bridge, with its seven semi-circular arches, was looked upon as one of the most remarkable structures in Scotland. It was approached in medieval times by the old road from the south—Causey Mounth, which was laid with Aberdeen stone cassies—hence its name.

William Elphinstone and Gavin Dunbar, Bishops of Aberdeen, are given the credit for ordering the bridge to be built and completed. Consequently their coat of arms, along with those of the city, the Regent Albany, who governed Scotland on behalf of the boy King James V, and various other inscriptions 28 in all—are to be seen on the buttresses of the upstream side.

A small clump of trees can be seen at the north-east end of the bridge, these mark the site of the chapel containing the silver bedecked figure of the Virgin Mary—Our Lady of Bon Accord. In 1560, during the Reformation, the chapel was ransacked and the statue thrown into the river.

Tradition has it that the wooden remains were picked up by a Flemish (Belgian) ship and taken to Brussels. There it stands to this very day, in the Notre Dame de Finistere. A replica can be seen in St Peter's Chapel, Castlegate, Aberdeen.

Over 450 years have pased since All Fools Day, 1527, when the Bridge of Dee was completed and opened to traffic—long may it stand!

The Auld Brig O' Dee.

A close-up of some of the 28 inscriptions on the bridge.

PALACES FOR THE PEOPLE IN THE PEOPLE'S PARK

Anyone would need to be at least 25 years of age to remember this building. It was the Palm House, known better these days as the Winter Gardens, and it stood in the Duthie Park until it was damaged by gales and replaced by the present building in 1970.

Miss Elizabeth Crombie Duthie, who owned the nearby Ruthrieston estate, gifted the ground to the city 110 years ago in 1880.

The main part of the gift comprised of Arthurseat, an estate which lay alongside the River Dee, and whose owner, A S Williamson, had totally disappeared.

There is at the entrance on Great Southern Road, a pleasing, turreted lodge house, once occupied by the park supervisor. Its twin can be seen on Anderson Drive, where it was shifted when the new south road was being built in the 1930s.

A statue to the Greek goddess of health Hygeia, on top of a tall fluted column, and guarded at the base by four lions, commemorates Miss Duthie. She herself thought up the idea of having the tallest flagpole in North-east Scotland on top of the large mound in the grounds.

Then the idea was to have the statue of William Wallace placed there. Instead it was placed, in 1888, at the junction of Union Terrace and Rosemount Viaduct. If placed on the mound, its tremendous weight would have probably caused it to sink without trace!

In front of the present Winter Gardens stands the granite parapet removed from the south side of the Union Bridge, which was built over in 1964, blocking off a fine view of the city to the south.

Inside are the bronze beasts (Kelly's Cats) which stood on top of the parapet. They are based on the leopard supporters of the city's coat of arms.

A number of other nostalgic items can be seen in the Winter Gardens, including Alexander Fidler's Well.

The well was situated in Guild Street and was the watering place for the mighty horses of the Messrs Wordie and Mutter Howie. On the back is the inscription:

> *Water springs for Man and Beast,*
> *At your service I am here.*
> *Although six thousand years of age,*
> *I am caller, clean and clear.*

and then with typical Aberdeen parochialism

> *Erected for the inhabitants of the world.*

Mr Fidler's generosity did not go unrewarded, and it is claimed that he was given a fine pocket watch and chain to commemorate his gift to all mankind. Local wags, however, pointed out that the watch cost more than the well!

The Palm House . . . blown down in 1970.

GAN WIR AIN GAIT!

While most of us heave a sigh of relief when the Christmas and New Year festivities are safely behind us, others in the North and East of Scotland are preparing to begin their celebrations!

We take it for granted nowadays that December 25 is the birthdate of Jesus Christ in the first century AD—Anno Domini, the year of our Lord—but no one actually knows.

The early Christians celebrated Christmas (the Mass of Christ) on dates as wide apart as the 1st and 6th of January, the 29th of March or the 29th of September. The firm date of 25th December seems to have come from Pope Julius in the 4th Century AD and has continued ever since.

It's to the Romans that we owe our present European custom of starting a New Year on the first day of the first month of the year—January.

In 45BC, the Emperor Julius Caesar devised a new calendar, known as the Julian Calendar. He named the first month, January, in honour of Janus, the god who looked after the doors and gates of the Roman heaven. Janus is always shown as having two faces—one looking in, and one looking out. Hence he could look forward to the new year and backward to the old one.

But Julius also made other changes which still linger with us to this day. He realised that the earth takes slightly more than 365 days to turn full circle, so he introduced an additional day every fourth year (a Leap Year). Unfortunately the solar year is actually short of this by 11¼ minutes.

Accordingly, the Julian Calendar was, by the 16th century, inaccurate by 10 days. Steps were taken by the then Pope, Gregory XIII, to remedy matters by eliminating the surplus days from his new Gregorian Calendar.

When Britain adopted this new style calendar in 1752, the missing 11 days were simply ignored, especially here in the North-east of Scotland.

The local people still remembered the Auld Yule (Aul' Eel) for many centuries, and in fact, in the Buchan area, Christmas—by the Julian Calendar, 5th January—is still celebrated on that day!

Going even further back to pagan times is the custom of lighting fires in the dead of winter to encourage the sun to return in the spring.

The locals at Stonehaven burn out the Old Year with fireballs. This is a most spectacular ceremony with the blazing balls being swung in great fiery arcs as they're paraded along the main street of the old town.

New Year's Eve (old style) is held at Burghead on 11th January, when they have the Burning of the Clavie, another ancient fire ritual. Although now confined to Burghead, there is evidence that up to a century ago, something similar took place in other east coast fishing ports.

Finally, the end of the festivities of Yule (old style)—Twenty-Fourth Night (29th January)—is held at Lerwick, with the splendid fire festival of Up-Helly-Aa.

I suppose here in the North East, we jist like tae gan wir ain gait!

Burning out the Old Year at Stonehaven.

35

EUROPE'S DASHING BLUE TOON LOON

This story begins in Peterhead, often called the Blue Toon—a name believed to have originated from the fisherfolk's practice of wearing woollen stocking feet over shoes; blue moggans these were called.

In Broad Street, as can be seen in the photograph, there's a statue of a gentleman in 18th century clothes holding a field marshal's baton, resplendent in knee-breeches, boots with spurs, and a three-cornered cocket hat.

This statue is the likeness of James Francis Edward Keith, born at Inverugie Castle near Peterhead, the youngest brother of the 10th and last Earl Marischal.

In 1715, at the age of 19, James took part with his father, the 9th Earl, in the first Jacobite Rising, led by The Old Pretender—Bonnie Prince Charlie's father.

The rebels raised their standard at Braemar at the place now occupied by the Invercauld Arms Hotel.

Under the leadership of the Earl of Mar were many other well-known North-east names, such as Farquharson of Invercauld, Black Jock of Invernan, the Marquis of Huntly, Gordon o' Glenbuchat, the Earl of Kintore, Irvine of Drum, the Frasers from Lonmay and Inverallochy, Lord Pitsligo, and Earl of Erroll.

They were opposed by the Government army led by the Duke of Argyll, and the two armies met at Sheriffmuir on the road to Stirling.

Both sides later claimed they'd trounced the other, but neutral observers saw it as a draw. The minister at Crathie Church, near Braemar, later wrote a comical verse about the battle.

Part of it goes:

> "There's some say that we won,
> And there's some say that they won,
> And some say that nane won at a' man
> But there's one thing that I'm sure
> That at Sheriffmuir,
> A battle there was, which I saw, man:
> An' we ran, an' they ran, an' they ran,
> An' we ran,
> An' we ran, an they ran, awa, man."

James Keith, in fact, ran awa to the continent. He became a colonel in the Spanish army but, not being a Catholic, his chances of promotion were pretty slim, so he travelled right across Europe and joined the Russian army.

Promotion was rapid in the ranks of the Czar, and James became a general. But as he was not a native-born Russian again his ambitions were limited. So he went on to Prussia—a state now integrated into Germany—where he became a Field Marshal and Governor of Berlin.

He was killed in 1758 in a battle between the Prussians and the Austrians at the village of Hochkirchen and buried there with full military honours. Later his body was exhumed and reinterred in Berlin's Garrison Church.

Just over a century later, in 1868, Kaiser William I presented Peterhead with the statue in remembrance of a brave Scotsman who died fighting for Prussia.

Once, when General Keith was fighting for the Russians against the Turks in the Crimea, a local truce was arranged, and Keith, in the full uniform of a Russian general, met his opposite number for talks.

The Turkish general was a magnificent figure in a dazzling suit, his silk turban encrusted with precious jewels. He had a swarthy complexion, dark piercing eyes and a luxurious black beard.

Both Keith and the Turk negotiated their business through interpreters. On reaching an understanding they both saluted and prepared to depart.

The Turk had been watching Keith closely throughout the whole proceedings, and, just as the Russian general was turning away, he laid his hand on James' arm.

"Hey min," he said. "You dinna ken me div ye? You're the loon Keith frae Peterhead, aren't ye? Well, I'm the bell-ringer's loon frae the Bullers o' Buchan.

"Ye've deen affa weel wi' the Rooskies, an I've deen nae bad wi' the Turks.

"Cheerio," he added—and off he went.

Which proves, as my mother used to say: "Agan' fit aye gets."

James Keith—honoured by the Kaiser of Germany.

36

STORMY WEATHER FOR AULD NICK'S CRONIES

Hallowe'en nowadays is a children's festival when they go guising from door to door, offering entertainment in return for gifts of money. Dooking for apples and carrying neepy lanterns is all part of the fun.

But October 31, the eve of All Saints Day, certainly wasn't looked upon as a fun day some centuries ago. Then, Hallowe'en was associated with witches, divination rites, and a general fear of the powers of darkness.

And at the very spot shown in this photograph, Aberdeen's witches were burned at the stake. So great was the attraction of a "roastin", that ropes had to be used to keep the spectators at bay!

In case your knowledge of Aberdeen is a bit hazy, go down Union Street to the Castlegate at its east end. Take the street to the left of the Salvation Army Citadel—this is Justice Street, called after the Justice Port (or gate), which stood here until some 200 years ago. Turn first right and you've arrived in Commerce Street—beneath your feet is the once grassy hollow lying between Castle Hill and the Heading Hill.

Here, so-called witches—in reality probably harmless auld wifies who appeared strange to their neighbours, and therefore undesirable, were tied to stakes, strangled and burned to ashes. The total bill for burning 23 witches in 1596 came to three pounds, three shillings and four pence.

The alleged witches came from all over the North-east—Kincardine O'Neil, Abergeldie, Blelack, Coull and even as far away as Glendye. An especial meeting place was reputed to be between the Brig O'Potarch and the village of Torphins, where on the lower slopes of Craiglash Hill there still stands a great muckle steen, known as the Warlock's Stone.

Witch-hunting really began in Scotland when King James VI set off on a voyage to Denmark to claim his royal bride, Anne. On their return a great storm blew up! James was puzzled by this unseasonal weather until a report reached him that an Edinburgh schoolteacher, Dr John Cunningham had confessed that he and 200 other witches and warlocks had put to sea in eggshells and sieves in order to create a storm to drown the king.

They had done this after listening to a sermon preached by the devil himself! Auld Nick had said that James was his worst enemy and had to be destroyed. This news pleased the king and caused a wave of witch-searching by his loyal subjects.

It was a blow to the credulous and pious when the Act against witchcraft was abolished in 1736. But even today some people like to have a horse-shoe above their door, or a rowan tree in their garden, to protect themselves against witches. Or perhaps they repeat the old prayer:

From ghoulies and ghosties and
long-leggety beasties
And things that go bump in the night,
Good Lord, deliver us!

Where witches were burned at the stake.

MURDER AT THE MILL

At the top of the Preston Tower, one of the five great towers of Fyvie Castle, which I wrote about some pages back, stands a small stone statue of a trumpeter. Legend has it that he's the Laird of Fyvie's trumpeter, Andrew Lambe, forever blowing his trumpet towards the Mill O' Tifty.

Andrew's sweetheart was named Agnes (Nan) Smith, but she was known far and wide as Mill O' Tifty's Annie. She lived with her father William, the miller, her mother, Helen and the rest of the family at the mill near the castle.

Once a year the Laird of Fyvie would make a tour of his estates and each family would stand at the door of their property to see the great man pass. During one of his annual visits, the Laird stopped his coach at the door of the Mill O' Tifty to compliment the miller on his fine family but especially to note how Annie had grown to be a beautiful 17-year-old girl.

Annie paid little heed to the Laird's fine words. She had eyes only for the Laird's trumpeter, Andrew Lambe. He sat there so handsome in his fine uniform, holding his silver trumpet. Annie thought him wonderful!

Soon their friendship grew. As often as they could, Annie would slip out of the mill and Andrew would leave his master's castle. The sweethearts met at a small bridge, which is still there, halfway between the mill and the castle.

One night, Annie's father, returning home, saw the pair together. A terrible scene followed, with Annie being forbidden to see Andrew again. For her father had a better match in mind for his daughter than a common trumpeter—maybe even the Laird himself.

From that day on, Annie was confined to the mill. But love laughs at locksmiths, and every so often she would slip out and meet Andrew who tried to console her and promise her a bright future. But the day came when he had to tell his sweetheart that all their hopes were dashed—he had to go to Edinburgh with his master for an indefinite period. They said their last farewells on the little brig and Annie went back, broken-hearted, to the Mill O' Tifty.

Weeks and months went by, and with no news from Andrew she began to pine and grew thin and pale. She was unable to do her household chores and her parents, guessing what was amiss, began to berate her.

At last one day, in a terrible fit of rage, as the song tells us, her father struck her—
"Wonderous sore, as also did her mither. An' broke her back at the Ha' door. For love o' Andrew Lambe". She lay there, crying for her Andrew, until she died.

You can see Annie's 300-year-old grave in Fyvie churchyard, with a simple inscription, "Annie Smith—Tifty's Annie".

The original had a crack across it—just like the crack on Annie's back—or so the locals used to say!

And Andrew Lambe? "The rest is silence."

Fyvie Castle—where Andrew Lambe blew for his Laird and his love!

DOWNIE'S DOWNFALL AND THE JOLLY STUDENTS' JAPE

Against this wall of King's College Chapel, the University Library at one time stood. And it was within its walls some two centuries ago, that the students became, "airt and pairt o' Downie's slaughter!"

For the students, unlike nowadays, had to live within the college. But students even then resented having restrictions placed on them.

The college authorities made plain their limits by marking the street to the south—College Bounds—as it is today.

Usually, the person who knew most about the students' movements was the college official who held the post of sacrist. George Downie was a sacrist during the 18th century. He was very unpopular, as the students believed, rightly or wrongly, that he was responsible for the punishments they had received for leaving the bounds.

One night, the professors and lecturers were invited to a dinner in the city. Off they went, leaving sacrist Downie alone with the students. The students dragged George from his office near the gate to the college library. There they held a mock trial and after due deliberation found the sacrist guilty!

Downie was taken to a side room where there was a block for his head, a basket of sawdust in front of it, and a masked executioner thoughtfully fingering the edge of an axe.

The sacrist was told that when the chapel clock struck eight, the axe would fall. On the eighth stroke, Downie closed his eyes as the axe was raised and his head placed on the block. The blow came. But it was only the slap of a cold, wet towel—the climax of the student prank!

However, the joke misfired as sacrist Downie died of a heart attack on the spot. The panic-stricken students hid the body and took an oath that no one would tell the truth until they knew they were the last person left alive who knew of Downie's execution.

Thus, many years passed before the disappearance of George Downie was solved.

There is a monument to the sacrist, near the Wallace Tower in Tillydrone. On it are the words: "Downie's Cairn, formerly associated with the tale of Downie the Sacrist. Stood at one time at Berryden. In 1926 was moved to this site."

Over the years, many people have asked if this story is true. I can only repeat the words on the monument—"I cannot tell how the truth may be, I say this tale as 'twas said to me."

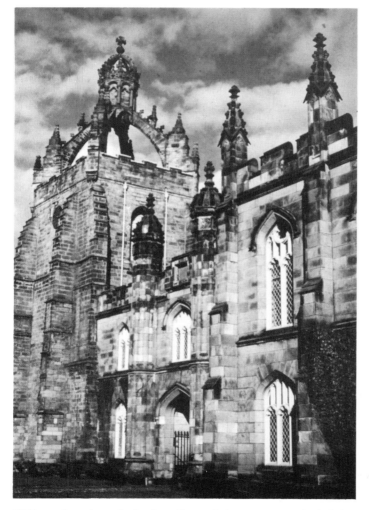

"When the chapel clock strikes eight, the axe will fall!"

The quad at King's, where the library once stood.

In memory of Downie's slaughter!

FREEDOM LANDS OF THE PEOPLE

How many people have walked past this memorial well and wondered what it was?

It is situated on the outskirts of Hazlehead Park and was built in 1884 to commemorate William Rose, Laird of Hazlehead, who moved into the estate in 1775 and built a mansion house there.

But he was only one of a line of private owners who, for 369 years, feued the estate from its real owners—the Town Council of Aberdeen!

The story properly begins in 1319 when King Robert the Bruce gave his Stocket Forest to the citizens of Aberdeen for the help they had given him in the War of Independence, culminating in the victory at Bannockburn in 1314. As the Aberdonians now paid no rent to the Crown, the area was known as the Freedom Lands, and the money which accrued from leasing out the property was known as the Common Good Fund.

However in 1551, certain leading Burgesses in the Burgh secured estates for themselves in the Freedom Lands at very advantageous terms. Hazlehead for example was acquired by the Chalmers family at a feu duty of £13 6s 8d. Then the Mortimers moved in and finally the Roses who occupied it until 1920.

In 1920 the Town Council decided to buy back its own property at a cost of £40,000 to establish a public park, golf courses and recreation facilities which now enhance the area.

Former owners are remembered in the names of the streets and tower blocks of the Hazlehead housing estate—Mortimer and Rose—while Scotland's heroes are not forgotten in Wallace and Bruce.

William Rose's stately mansion was taken down in 1960 to be replaced by the existing restaurant. As the visitor walks from the main gate past the old fashioned cottage built in 1826—and once the home of the head gardener—towards the restaurant, they should note the three Redwood trees which were planted to celebrate the birth of each of the daughters of a Rose family owner. The girls, according to tradition, are also remembered in the names of the surrounding fields—Maryfield, Bellfield and Jessiefield (the site of the city Crematorium).

Hazlehead Park is among the very small number of areas in Britain which can boast a maze. Hampton Court has one and it is thanks to a former Lord Provost, Sir Henery Alexander, who gifted it in 1935, that Aberdeen has one.

The Town Council of 1551 may have erred in leasing out the property to private owners, but the City Fathers of 1920 more than made up for their predecessors' lapse by buying back the land and opening it to its true owners—the citizens of Aberdeen. Take advantage of the Freedom Lands by visiting Hazlehead.

The 'mysterious' memorial well at Hazlehead Park.

FELLOWSHIP WAS GOOD AT CASTLEHILL

Mentioning Castlehill a few pages ago, brings to mind some details of the castle of Aberdeen which gave the hill its name.

Records regarding the castle are hard to come by. It is known that Edward I—the Hammer of Scots—saw the fortress in 1296 on his tour of Scotland and described it as "bon" or good. Aberdeen's first recorded Provost, Richard the Mason, certainly worked on the Castlehill. And the English King left a garrison there when he departed.

When Edward heard that Robert the Bruce had crowned himself King of Scots, he again planned to invade Scotland. However, he died, but before doing so he made his son, Edward, promise to carry his father's bones on the campaign.

But the Prince of Wales did not have the same determination as his father. He led the English army only as far as Ayrshire then turned back for home.

Tradition has it that when Edward II finally met with Robert the Bruce and the Scots army at Bannockburn, Aberdonians were among the army. Following the victory over the auld enemy, the citizens returned to the burgh determined to attack the English-held castle.

As they had to recognise each other in the dark, they used a password—bon accord—good fellowship. The attack was successful and to this day, Bon Accord is, of course, the motto of the city, and the three towers of the castle are on the coat-of-arms.

Apart from its mention in various documents and records, there is no description of the castle whatever—it seems as if it didn't exist for long. Its only real claim to fame is that it gave its name to the hill—Castlehill.

What did exist on Castlehill for many centuries was St Ninian's Chapel—which may have been the garrison church. Following the Reformation in the 1560s, the chapel was made into a sort of lighthouse, and three great burning lights were placed there each winter night for the guidance of mariners. These beacons were used for nearly 60 years.

The chapel was then used for a variety of purposes. It was a mortuary chapel, a courthouse, a gunpowder store and a prison!

Near to it, Oliver Cromwell's men built a small fort, of which a corner can still be seen at the junction of Castle Terrace with Commerce Street.

Two hundred years ago, the chapel was demolished when the Castlehill was leased to the Government. On its site was built the Castlehill Barracks, for long the depot of the Gordon Highlanders. I'm sure some of the older readers can remember seeing the soldiers on guard in their red jackets, Gordon tartan kilts and feathered bonnets, outside the gates.

In 1935, the Gordons moved to the Bridge of Don. The old barracks were finally pulled down 30 years later to make way for two skyscraper blocks.

But would King Edward I some 800 years on, have described the present group of buildings on Castlehill as "bon"?

'A Gordon for me!'

RUGGED BEAUTY THAT INSPIRED DRACULA

When visitors to Cruden Bay see the ruins of Slains Castle and hear how the author of the Dracula stories used to holiday in the area, they naturally assume that he was inspired by the rugged coastline and imagined the blood-sucking Count Dracula sleeping deep in the ruins of the Castle.

But really the castle didn't look like this until 15 years after the originator of Dracula died, and although like millions of other people they enjoy (or are horrified by) the Prince of Darkness and his blood curdling actions, they don't know anything at all about the man who created him, or even his name!

His name was Bram—short for Abraham—Stoker, and he was an Irishman from Dublin. He began his adult working life as a civil servant but soon gave that up and became the manager of Sir Henry Irving, the famous actor.

Bram Stoker came to the Cruden Bay area just about 100 years ago, when he was on holiday in Peterhead. He was fond of walking and one August day in 1893 he set off along the coast. After about eight miles he came to Cruden Bay, known at that time as Port Errol.

Stoker was enchanted with the place. He looked for a house to stay in, and finally decided to stay in the local hotel, the Kilmarnock Arms, which is still there.

Dracula was written during the time Bram holidayed in the area. In fact other stories were also written during successive stays. The Mystery of The Sea (1902) has its hero staying in the Kilmarnock Arms, and the action is set three miles south of Whinnyfold—Finny-fa to the locals. It is obvious that Stoker came to know the area well.

Most people have never heard of The Mystery of the Sea or anything else the Irishman wrote about the area. But not only did Bram get to know the coastline well, he also used the local dialect in another story—The Watter's Mou, a romantic tale of Willie, a young coastguard, in love with Maggie a fisherman's daughter.

Alas, Maggie's father is also a smuggler in his spare time and Maggie has to make a desperate dash through the raging seas to warn her father that the coastguards are waiting for him. Worse follows—the boat overturns and Willie has to plunge into the cruel sea in an attempt to save her. Both are drowned. The two corpses, wrapped in each others arms, are washed ashore—at The Watter's Mou.

A real Dracula touch that—not one corpse, but two! And probably you're wondering whether Bram Stoker got his inspiration for the Prince of Darkness from someone he met while on holiday? Well, not really: the idea came from guide books, and research in various libraries—for Bram never went to Transylvania in his life.

If there was a Dracula, he was probably Prince Vlad Dracula the Vth of Wallachia (present-day Romania). The prince lived from 1431 to 1476, near Bucharest. Even in a blood-thirsty age, Vlad was exceptional—when some visiting noblemen forgot to take off their hats in his presence, the Prince ordered his soldiers to nail the visitors' hats to their heads.

In 1931, five hundred years after his death, Dracula's tomb was opened—and found to be empty!

An original edition of Dracula today is worth many hundreds of pounds. But the author never knew how successful it was to be. It was some 20 years after Stoker's death that Bela Lugosi made Dracula famous on the screen. 50 years later, it's still guaranteed to give cinemagoers the shivers.

Younger readers associate Christopher Lee with the role in numerous Hammer Horror films. But there are many other versions of Dracula with around 400 films on the subject.

What would Bram Stoker have thought about it all as he sat in his Cruden Bay holiday digs whiling away the time with his scribblings? As a theatrical manager I'm sure he would have been delighted!

By the way—how did the castle fall into ruins some 15 years after the author's death?

Well, that's another story for another page!

The grim coastline below Slains Castle.

THE SANDS OF TIME

Who would imagine that a peaceful area, as depicted by these sand dunes, could cause the River Findhorn to burst its banks and sweep away the old village nearby!

All this happened some three hundred years ago and the damage was not done by a sea of water, but by a sea of sand, which poured millions of tonnes of grains on to the land, burying the ground to a depth of two to three feet!

Eighteen years later, in 1694, another sandstorm hit the area so suddenly that reapers and harvesters in the fields had to abandon their tools and flee for their lives. Clouds of choking particles filled the air, entering people's mouths and lungs.

A sand-drift, like a wide, slowly-moving river, flowed steadily over the Culbin area, near Forres, covering everything in its path.

Soon there was nothing of Culbin to be seen except a desert of sand some five miles long by two miles wide—a whole village complete with mansion house and outlying farms all disappeared!

Actually, there's some mystery as to what really happened. Some versions of the story say it all happened overnight—others blame a series of storms—but the superstitious had no doubt—it was the work of the Devil!

Anyway, the Laird of Culbin was to blame—the fairer-minded among his people agreed that they should never have been asked to take in the harvest on the Sabbath—the day of rest!

The unco-guid claimed that the Laird, a notorious gambler, had been playing cards with Auld Nick and had lost—hence the reason for the entire village being swept away to Hell.

To be fair, it's a well-known fact that sand needs to be held down somehow, or it will drift about freely. Nature does the job wonderfully well with marram grass—that's the long, tough grass you find near the sea-shore.

Unfortunately, the workers of Culbin used to cut this grass steadily and use it to thatch their cottage roofs. Without the grass, the sand was free to drift about.

Scotland's Parliament recognised the problem, and passed an Act banning the use of marram grass for roof-thatching—a law which was probably totally ignored by the locals!

If you go to the Culbin Sands area today, you'll see the wonderful work in planting trees which the Forestry Commission has done over some 60 years.

Most of the sand is now established but every now and again there's a shift and perhaps a chimney-pot might be uncovered.

I wouldn't shout down it if I were you—there could be an unexpected cry for help—or an invitation to play a hand of cards—the game of course being "Deil tak the hindmaist!"

A sea . . . of sand!

THEY CANNAE STEAL A MARCH ON US

Many visitors to Aberdeen, as well as locals, have asked me to explain to them certain peculiarly shaped and marked stones, which are to be found in, and around, the City. These stones, one of which is pictured here, mark the Freedom Lands and Privileges of the City and Royal Burgh of Aberdeen.

And they are well worth watching, for they mark the boundaries (the Marches) of the land given to the City by King Robert I—the Bruce—in 1319. Nowadays, the generous gift of the King is valued at £20,000,000!

There are 67 such stones. The first one is at the side of the River Dee, between Queen Victoria Bridge and Queen Elizabeth Bridge and is the Alpha stone. The last one is on the Don between the new bridge and the sea and is, appropriately, the Omega stone.

As can be seen from the photograph each stone has on it ABD for Aberdeen and its number. If it stands on the boundaries of the ancient Royal Burgh it is further marked CR for City Royalty (or property).

March Stones are either totally overlooked or are mistaken for old milestones! For example, No 3 at the corner of Nellfield Place, is so close to No 4, just a few yards away in Great Western Road, that people thought it a short mile—hence the origin of the name of the local hostelry!

Over the hundreds of years which the town has held the Freedom Lands, their right to it has been challenged a number of times. One example was when James IV, in debt to his Admiral Sir Andrew Wood of Largo in Fife, bestowed on him the Stocket Forest. When the bold sailor anchored off Girdleness, early one morning in 1494, the citizens were waiting for him. The prudent Sir Andrew set sail for home, leaving his prize unclaimed.

Thus for centuries, canny Aberdonians have safeguarded their gift from Robert the Bruce.

Aware of the "siller in the civic pooch", they have made it their duty to repel any unwarranted interference by outside bodies to encroach on the City's ancient privileges.

Long may such watchfulness flourish—Bon Accord!

The Omega March Stone at the Bridge of Don.

46

BEWARE THE MIDS O' MAR

After some fifty years Aberdeen's Castlegate has returned to its original purpose. For centuries until the 1930s, it was the market place for the Burgh.

The traders and merchants paid their fees, or tolls, at a stall or booth set up for the purpose. This building was therefore known as the Tolbooth. It was also used for meetings of the Town Council, as well as being handy as a lock-up for the town drunks and rascals on market days.

Edinburgh also had its Tolbooth or prison, known as the Heart of Midlothian—now demolished—but Aberdeen's own Mids o' Mar still exists, if you know where to find it! Between the Town House, and the bank on the corner of King Street, there is an archway—all that remains of Lodge Walk—and there can be seen the part of the Aberdeen Tolbooth, shown in this photograph.

The tall, fortress-like tower, is capped by a slender spire. The few small windows are heavily barred. Inside are still the iron-bound doors, massive bolts, chains and padlocks that probably have existed since the place was built in 1615. The condemned cell is the only original one still remaining in Scotland. Once a prisoner was sentenced to death he, or she, was then chained to a long iron bar, permanently fixed to the floor of the cell. With all these precautions it seems impossible that anyone could escape from such a place. Incredible as it seems, a number of people did get free. The best known of them was Peter Young, a well-known Caird—tinker or gypsy—from Dundee.

Peter's father was James "Gypsy" Young, and his mother was the daughter of Cockle-ee Graham. Cockle-ee was a force to be reckoned with, being a henchman of the infamous Rob Roy himself! At 15 Peter was caught red-handed breaking into a house in Tough, Aberdeenshire, but was lucky to get off with a thrashing. He drew no lessons from his failure, however, and along with his brother, Robert, bungled another break-in.

This time both brothers were seized and lodged in the Aberdeen Tolbooth. Peter was endowed with remarkable cunning and made up a paste which he spread on their bodies until they looked as if they had some horrible infectious skin disease. The authorities removed them to an isolation area from which they easily escaped.

By the time he was 18, Peter was a married man. He married his cousin Jean, but did not settle down to be a model of domesticity. For the happy couple immediately embarked on a life of joint crime. Following a number of offences in Banff, Portsoy and Turriff, Peter and Jean were captured, and for a second time Peter was a prisoner in the Mids o' Mar. This time he was sentenced to death, as was Jean. However, it was discovered that she was pregnant so the date of her execution was postponed until after the baby's birth.

But once again Peter's criminal ingenuity came to the fore, and with the aid of outside help, he manufactured a set of keys and walked out of the Tolbooth, with his wife Jean. At the same time, to show his generous nature, he released all the other prisoners!

Three months later the couple were re-captured, and this time Peter was bound in yards of chains and sent to the Heart of Midlothian in Edinburgh. There, at the age of 22, he was hanged. On that very day, in the Tolbooth, Aberdeen, Jean gave birth to their child.

Less than two months later, she too met her husband's fate, on the gallows erected in front of the Tolbooth.

Have a look at a square of granite cassies set into the tarmacadam, just before the traffic lights at the corner of Castle Street and King Street. It was on that spot that Mrs Peter Young, wife and mother, met her untimely end.

Still standing grim and strong—the Tolbooth as seen from Lodge Walk.

TALL TALES OF OUR TOWER OF BABBLE

Most Aberdonians can tell you that this picturesque building is the Wallace Tower, and that it is situated at Tillydrone. Older citizens can recall before the 1960s when it was a public house; standing at the junction of Carnegie's Brae and Netherkirkgate. Ask why it's so-called and the usual reply is: "Well, that's Wallace standing there on the tower, his sword in his hand, and a dog at his feet."

To reinforce Wallace's connection with the city, there's a huge statue of him in Rosemount Viaduct, erected just over 100 years ago.

And didn't he raid Dunnottar Castle, putting all the English to the sword, before coming to Aberdeen and burning their ships? Finally, when the Guardian of Scotland was hung,

Benholm's Lodging ... popularly known as the Wallace Tower. Displaced from the Netherkirkgate by Marks and Spencers.

drawn, and quartered in London, wasn't one of his legs sent to the city and put on display near St Machar's Cathedral?

Now, if you've believed all of these legends about Wallace and his exploits here in the North-east, I'm sorry to tell you that there are no contemporary Scottish writers, nor independent English records, who mention these stories at all!

Most of the Wallace legend comes from verses in praise of him by a poet or minstrel, Blind Harry, who was writing 150 years after the events.

Officially, the Wallace Tower is Benholm's Lodging, and its nickname, first coined in the 1790s, comes from the fact that it stood near one of the city wells. The well-house tower, became the well-'ouse, and then the Wallace Tower.

And that statue? Well, it's that of Sir Robert Keith of Benholm (south of Stonehaven) who built the Tower in about 1600—and that's 300 years after William Wallace! Sir Robert's brother, George, founded Marischal College later in the century.

Incidentally, Wallace's limbs were sent to Newcastle, Berwick, Perth and Stirling, while his head was displayed on London Bridge.

As Robbie Burns once said: "Facts are chiels that winna ding" and whatever tales Aberdonians may have woven around Benholm's Lodging and William Wallace over the centuries, we're not free to tell fanciful stories we think our children or visitors might like to hear. When Henry Ford suggested that "history is bunk" perhaps he'd been speaking to an American just back from a visit to the city!

Sir Robert Keith, who lived some 300 years after William Wallace.

GRIM AND GLORIOUS MARISCHAL STREET

"He'll finish up lookin' doon Marischal Street," was a grim Aberdonian prophecy that a wicked person would hang outside the Castlegate Tolbooth. The victim's last view of the world would be the street directly opposite the scaffold.

Compared to its close neighbours, the Castlegate or the Shiprow—800-years-old—Marischal Street is not really old. Built over 200 years ago as a new approach to the harbour area, its making removed one of the most impressive medieval houses in the city—the Earl Marischal's House.

The Keith family, with its imposing fortress at Dunnottar near Stonehaven, was hereditary Marischal—or Keeper of the King's Peace—of Scotland. The Keiths' town house had seen a lot of history since its construction about 1540.

From one of its windows the 19-year old widow, Mary Queen of Scots, was forced to witness the execution of Sir John Gordon by the Aberdeen version of the guillotine, The Maiden, following the battle of the Corrichie Burn in 1562.

In the same house, in 1716, the Jacobite leaders decided to give up their struggle against "the wee wee German Lairdie", George I, who was now their king. The Earl Marischal went into exile with the Old Pretender, and from Berlin agreed to sell his house for the handsome sum of £800, to make way for a new street to be named after him—Marischal Street.

Looking down the street, there can be seen on the west side the Elim Tabernacle, or Pentecostal Church, which marks the site of the old Theatre Royal or, as it was known to Aberdonians, The Band Box.

The builder of this side of the street was William "Sink-'em" Smith, father of the first Aberdeen City Architect, "Tudor Johnny" Smith, and grandfather of the second City Architect, William "Balmoral" Smith.

Halfway up the street was Bannerman's Bridge, now demolished to make way for the dual carriageway in Virginia Street below.

The street was a fashionable residential quarter in its heyday. Still visible are Georgian doorways with fanlight windows over them. Some of the doors are high and wide so that a sedan-chair could be taken into the house.

Many famous Aberdonians lived in Marischal Street, including several provosts and the famous artist, William Dyce. Such history is often forgotten, but Aberdeen is lucky in having a number of societies whose aim is to keep alive our local heritage—long may they remain active!

The site of the gallows and the last view for many.

THE GRANITE QUEEN OF ABERDEEN

If Marischal College is the King building of the Silver City, then the Town House—shown in this photograph—must be the Queen.

Curiously enough, when the plans for a new Town House were being discussed in the 1860s, it was felt it would have to be built in red brick, as there wasn't enough granite readily available in the area for such a large project!

However, the owner of Kemnay quarries, 15 miles from Aberdeen, guaranteed that he would deliver all the granite needed—and he certainly kept his word!

There has been a Town House or Tolbooth on the same site for 600 years since Robert III granted the Burgesses a licence to build one anywhere in the area except in the middle of the Castlegate!

Probably the first Provost to preside over the council meetings in the new premises was Robert Davidson, who was to be killed at Harlaw in 1411. The Provost was carried back to the city on his shield and buried in the Mither Kirk—St Nicholas.

During rebuilding of the church about 250 years ago, Davidson's grave was opened and a small silk cap, which he had worn, was found. But the skull-cap, tomb and the inscription above it on the wall, have all disappeared. Tradition has it that since the time of "guide Sir Robert", no Lord Provost of Aberdeen is allowed to officially leave the city.

Some 200 years after the first Tolbooth was built, severe gales damaged it so badly that a new one was erected in 1615. Its lead-covered spire and clock tower can be seen to the right of the photograph.

This Tolbooth eventually proved to be too cramped and in 1750 a completely new Town House was built on the site which had been used for so long. It was attached to the old Tolbooth which was now named the High Tolbooth and the new building, the Laigh (or low) Tolbooth.

It was described as plain and unremarkable with five large windows looking on to the market place.

Just over a hundred years ago in 1870, the present Town House was built. If you feel the design has a European or Flemish look to it, then blame the architects who came from Edinburgh and were chosen to do the work despite the presence of several very capable local architects.

The most notable feature of the Town House is the clock tower which is 190ft high.

Although the Laigh Tolbooth of 1750 is gone, one relic of it remains in view. It is the metal sundial which can be seen on the wall beneath the High Tolbooth tower, at the end of the granite facade. On it is the Latin inscription which sums up the 600 years of Town House existence—Ut umbra sic vita fugit—Like a shadow, life flies.

The Town House, Aberdeen. 600 years of civic government on the same site.

THE TRAVELS OF THOMAS-SAN

When Puccini's world famous opera, Madame Butterfly, is performed on the stage in Aberdeen, it's a matter of bringing coals to Newcastle.

For it can be claimed that the whole story began in the city. Or, to be really accurate, at the Bridge of Don.

The superintendent of the Coastguard Station there, 150 years ago, was a retired Naval officer, Lieutenant Glover. His son young Tom had been born in Fraserburgh and, after being educated at the Old Aberdeen Gymnasium School, he set out in 1857 to make his fortune and landed in Japan, then ruled by the Shogun.

Thomas Blake Glover, who became known as the Scottish Samurai, prospered in Japan, marrying a local girl and building a large bungalow on the coast road outside Nagasaki. It faced the Mitsubishi shipyards which he had founded.

Yet Glover did not forget he was an Aiberdeen loon. In 1868, when the Japanese Navy was founded, Tom persuaded the country's government to go to the shipyard of Alexander Hall, thousands of miles away in Footdee, to have its first battleship built.

50 years later, his son continued the Aberdeen connection by also having a trawler (or Smoky Joe) constructed by the Aberdeen workforce for the Japanese fishing industry.

Some years after Glover's death, Puccini became intrigued by this love affair between East and West, ancient and modern, and wanted to show that in a clash of cultures something had to give. Madame Butterfly, one of the most popular of all operas, was the result.

Unlike the Puccini's hero Leiutenant Pinkerton, however, Thomas Glover was a faithful and loving husband to his Japanese wife for some 30 years.

Following Glover's death in 1911, his son, also named Tom, lived on in Nagasaki and was one of the survivors of the dropping of the atomic bomb there in 1945. Shortly afterwards, however, possibly afraid that he might be regarded as a war criminal by the occupying Allied Forces, Tomisaburo Glover committed suicide.

The Madame Butterfly opera only goes to show that often truth is stranger than fiction!

Tom Glover's boyhood home—Braehead, Bridge of Don.

Thomas Blake Glover—the Scottish Samurai.

A Japanese 'Butterfly'.

THE DAY THE DRUMDURNO MAID MADE A DEAL WITH THE DEVIL

At the beginning of this book I wrote about stone circles in the North-east and how various theories have been suggested as to their use.

Much mystery surrounds the so-called Pictish symbol stones, an excellent example of which can be seen in this photograph of the Maiden Stone at Chapel of Garioch, near Inverurie.

The Picts received their name from the Roman invaders, who gave them the title from the Latin word for painted— the natives being in the habit of covering their bodies in designs before going into battle.

Pictland was all of the area north of the River Forth, and the Romans penetrated the heartland when they came from Raedykes, near Stonehaven, and crossed the North-east to Burghead on the Moray Firth, via Peterculter, Kintore and Ythanwells.

There is little trace of the Picts except in place-names, few examples of their writing on stone, called Ogam script, and the wonderful sculpted stones only to be found in Scotland, and even there mostly in Pictland—that is North-east Scotland around the Garioch.

Historians do not agree on what the carvings mean. Some maintain that the designs are symbols of authority—others that they signify the achievements of the person they commemorate—but it is obvious that the later ones have a strong connection with the coming of Christianity to the area.

For example, at the bottom half of the Maiden Stone in the picture is supposed to be a whale, connecting it with the story of Jonah!

Whatever the truth of the matter, the locals will tell you that the Maiden Stone is a relic of Janet Maitland, the Maid of Drumdurno. Janet was beautiful, and one day was busy baking. Suddenly she became aware of a handsome young stranger on the doorstep. Soon they were chatting away like old friends. He quickly praised her cooking and, having tasted one of her bannocks, laughingly asked if she would marry him! Janet teased him in return and, looking through the open door, pointed to Bennachie in the distance.

"If you can make a path from the Mither Tap there to my mother's door before tea-time, I'll fairly marry ye!" she said. The young man said nothing and disappeared as quickly as he had come.

Janet continued to busy herself about the house. As tea-time approached she went to the kitchen door to look for her family. To her amazement and growing horror, she saw a path had been laid from the Mither Tap and was rapidly coming to her door! Janet realised, too late, that the handsome stranger had really been Auld Nick himself in disguise, and that she had struck a bargain with him.

The Maid of Drumdurno ran to escape but she was too late—the Devil caught her by the shoulder and she turned to stone! There she stands to this very day.

As you can see from this photograph, at the bottom of the stone are the symbols of poor Janet—her mirror and her comb. The gap at the top of the stone is where her shoulder would have been.

And if you go there and look up the hill you'll still see the remains of the path which the Devil built from the top of Bennachie.

Of course, as I say, learned historians will tell you differently but we here in the North-east ken itherwise— divn't wi!

The Maiden Stone at the Chapel o' Garioch . . . a fine example of a Pictish symbol stone.

A wonderfully carved stone showing the connection between the Picts and Christianity.

WATERY TALE OF A WANDERING MANNIE

"Water, water everywhere. Nor any drop to drink" was the cry of the Ancient Mariner. And 300 years ago many Aberdonians must have echoed that sentiment.

At that time the water supply for the city came from the Loch of Aberdeen which is still remembered in the name Loch Street. In fact the street still has the curved shape it had when it ran alongside the loch.

The bed of the loch is now covered in by George Street and the Bon Accord Centre.

The taste of the water from the Loch was appalling even by 17th Century standards. A new, cleaner water supply was badly needed.

Various sources were tested and it was decided to take water from Carden Haugh (or valley) near the present day Grammar School, now remembered in Carden Place.

The water was kept in a reservoir at the Fountainhall wellhouse, now in the Duthie Park and piped downhill to the Castlegate where the famous wellhouse, with its little Mannie or statue on the top, was placed in 1708.

William Lindsay was the water overseer for the town council at this time and it was rumoured that as he was a goldsmith, the Mannie was to be be made of gold.

Then, said the gossips, it was to be made of brass and there were typical Aberdeen mutterings when it was discovered that it was cast in lead and painted in goldpaint.

Never-the-less, the Mannie has lasted nearly 200 years and in that time has seen some changes.

He stood in the Castlegate at the east end for 150 years. Then in 1852 he was shifted to the Green to become the Mannie in the Green—for another 100 years watching over the henwives and the fishwives selling their various products.

Finally, in 1972, he returned to his original home in the Castlegate, though this time to the west end.

Nowadays our water comes from the River Dee and is purified by the most modern methods. In 1967, the control of the town's water supply was taken from the City Fathers and passed to a regional water board.

In doing so it meant stories of the Invercannie Waterworks trips passed into legend and history.

Councillor George Roberts once recalled that in 1922 they were conveyed in Rolls Royce taxis to the site, and had lunch in a specially erected marquee by the river.

The fine food being, of course, washed down not by purified Dee water but by other stronger beverages.

Unfortunately the Mannie Well is now dry which brings us back full circle.

The much-travelled Mannie . . . back in the Castlegate.

THE LAST TRAM HOME

A way of life disappeared on the 3rd May 1958 when over 80 years of Aberdeen's tramway history came to an end.

The first trams were horse-drawn. Two lines operated in 1874, one line going from Queen's Cross to the North Church—the Arts Centre nowadays—and the other from the junction of Union Street and St Nicholas Street to Kittybrewster. Drivers and conductors worked fourteen and a half hours each day with an hour off for breakfast and dinner, but the horses worked a shorter day! The wages for a 72 hour week were £1.4/-.

Electrification came at the turn of the century, but the cost of the operation was such that no private company could afford it. Accordingly, the Corporation bought over the tramways, and electric traction began. The loyal horses, who were stabled at the corner of Baker Street and Rosemount, were put out to pasture.

Most people in the city travelled by public transport. In 1958, 100,000,000 passengers were carried by the Aberdeen Coporation Transport Department. However, even that was a drop of some 20,000,000 from 10 years earlier. The motor car was already taking its toll on public transport.

To carry such numbers of passengers, there were over 100 tramcars and 150 buses. The staff in 1958 worked a shorter week—44 hours—and had increased their wages to £9.11/1d. To travel up Union Street cost two old pennies, while Dee to Don was all of 5d!

Trams and buses were painted green and cream and each tram route had its own colour band painted around the top deck. For instance, Service No 1—Bridge of Dee to Bridge of Don—was red, while No 2 for Mannofield was dark brown.

For various reasons it was decided to abandon trams in favour of buses, and in 1951 the Mannofield route was changed over. 1954 saw the Rosemount service being withdrawn, and a year later Woodside became tramless. In 1956, Hazlehead and Sea Beach followed suit. The Bridges route was the last to go in 1958.

As befits the death of a lifetime friend, the citizens and Corporation gave the trams a grand send-off. A procession, led by one of the original horse-drawn trams, had the Chief Inspector on the platform. Behind came a line of other trams, both old and new. On the tram-lines, still to be seen near the Sea Beach, they were set on fire.

One of the reasons given for getting rid of trams was the argument that they slowed down the flow of vehicles. It is ironic, therefore, that a number of traffic-snarled cities are re-introducing modern, fast, trams. Is it a case of "come back, all is forgiven!"

From Dee to Don for 5d!

THE GREY GRANITE HAS A STORY TO TELL OF ITS OWN

Aberdonians like to tell visitors that Marischal College, as seen in this photograph, is one of the largest granite buildings in the world—but ask them where the granite came from and they generally change the topic!

As many prominent buildings in the city are made from granite, the term—The Granite City—seems to be so appropriate to Aberdeen, but it's really only over the last couple of centuries that the description has been true. The reason is that granite, naturally plentiful in this area, is very hard to fashion into building blocks, therefore most of the ordinary houses and even some of the landmarks were made from freestone. St Nicholas Church and Kings College are two such examples.

Despite the difficulty of using granite for building, there are in the North-east some very ancient granite buildings—Crathes and Drum Castles on Deeside, and Midmar with Castle Fraser on Donside, some of which date back eight centuries. In the city we have St Machar's Cathedral, nearly as old as these.

These early granite buildings were made from handy-sized boulders gathered from the seashore or carried from the fields to give the plough a chance to turn over the soil.

The drystane dykes at the edges of most fields in the countryside show how plentiful the supply was.

About 200 years ago, granite came into general use for building in the city, and probably the first quarry opened for the purpose was the Dancing Cairns, which in 1840 supplied the portico for the Music Hall, and the material for the statue of the Duke of Gordon in Golden Square. The statue is claimed to be the first of its kind since those of the Ptolemy's of Egypt many centuries ago.

Residents in Rosemount will be familiar with the names of Loanhead Terrace and Place, and they commemorate a quarry which once existed there.

Examples of Loanhead granite can be seen within the area at Robert Gordon's College, the Denburn Church in Summer Street, or the Old Infirmary in Woolmanhill.

But most of the buildings in the city came from the granite of Rubislaw Quarry, which has been described as "the hole which Aberdeen came out of!"

It wasn't just the locals who wanted Rubislaw granite—it was in great demand in London for paving the streets. They lifted all the wooden blocks in the capital's streets and replaced them with Aberdeen granite "cassies" or "setts". This was all done by hand, of course, by men called paviors, who dunted in the stones by sheer brute force!

So where does the granite for Marischal College come from? The answer is Kemnay. Other buildings in the town from the same source are the Town House, HM Theatre, and the Salvation Army Citadel, to name but a few.

We should be proud of our local stone which has gone all over the world. Some think it's too cold and colourless—but as Elvis used to say—"Don't knock the rock!"

Marischal College . . . an Aberdeen tourist attraction.

THE ARMS OF MONTROSE

'A shot . . . and the drummer-boy fell dead!'

Throughout the centuries Aberdeen and the North-east of Scotland have played a notable—and at times a leading role—not only in Scottish affairs, but in British events. One such occasion came about when King Charles I wanted to change the Presbyterian Church of Scotland to become more like the Episcopalian Church of England.

However, when the minister of St Giles Cathedral in Edinburgh began to conduct the new style of service, one of the congregation—Jenny Geddes—flung the stool she sat on at him and roared out: "Ye durna say the Mass at ma lug!"

Opposition grew and Scotland became split into those who supported the king and those who opposed him.

Those against the king signed a bond or covenant, and thus were called Covenanters. Those who supported the king were, naturally, Royalists.

The first shots of the Civil War which followed and lasted some dozen years were fired right here in the North-east!

The Royalist Gordon lairds of Haddo, Udny and Gight entered the town of Turriff—then a Covenanter stronghold, and defended by Sir William Hay of Delgaty. In this first battle the Royalists won—"nae bother at a!" A wee rhyme commemorates the event, nicknamed The Trot o' Turriff, it goes like this:

> *Historians say that at the Trot,*
> *The natives there a thrashin' got.*
> *They threw doon their weapons on the spot,*
> *An ran awa frae Turra!*

Eight year later in 1644, James Graham Marquis of Montrose, came to Aberdeen at the head of a Royalist army. They came from the south by way of the Cairn o' Mount, Peterculter, present-day Bieldside, Garthdee, and stopped, overlooking the city at the Twa-Mile Cross.

The Marquis sent a letter calling on the town to surrender. His missive can still be seen in the city archives with the curved lines of writing that came from using his saddle as a writing desk. A messenger under a white flag, accompanied by a drummer boy, carried the document to the city magistrates.

On their return, as they passed through the Green a shot rang out and the drummer boy fell dead! Montrose's men were determined to show no mercy for the flagrant breach of the flag of truce.

At the battle of the Hardgate which followed, the Aberdonians under the leadership of Balfour of Burleigh were no match for Royalist Highlanders. The wounded and the dying were taken to a little well, which is still there to this day—below Strawberry Bank, at the top of the Hardgate—its name: the Bloody Well!

Montrose was captured in 1649. He was hung, drawn and quartered and his head put on display in Edinburgh. Perth and Stirling were to have an arm each while one leg was to come to Glasgow and another to Aberdeen. Strangely enough, it was the Marquis's right arm which eventually came here.

The limb was nailed to the Tolbooth door in the Castlegate. There it remained until it was taken down and buried in St Nicholas Churchyard. 10 years later, Harry Graham (Montrose's brother) was allowed to collect the Marquis's remains together and bury them in St Giles in Edinburgh.

Some time ago, at a meeting of historians in Edinburgh, an Englishman from Yorkshire exhibited a dried and mummified arm, which had all the signs of being Montrose's arm, complete with the nail marks where it had been fixed to the door some 300 years before!

Perhaps some canny Aberdonian kept it as a relic and later sold it—or is that stretching the long arm of coincidence too far?

The Bloody Well in the Hardgate, where the water turned red!

EARL ERROLL'S EYRIE

Some pages back I wrote about Bram Stoker, the author of Dracula, and how he became connected with Slains Castle. At the end of the story I mentioned that a number of years after Stoker's death, the castle became a ruin, and promised to tell how this came about.

Many people think that Slains Castle is like Dunnottar further down the coast—an ancient ruin. But really, the ruins are not very old, most of them dating from 1830, when the 18th Earl of Erroll had it rebuilt.

The family name of the Earls of Erroll is Hay, and there are various stories as to how they received their name.

One of the more colourful stories concerns the Battle of Luncarty when the Scots under Kenneth III were fighting the Danes, and were forced to retreat through a narrow pass.

An old man and his two sons were ploughing nearby and came to help their fellow Scots. The three of them blocked the pass with their plough and took the yoke off the oxen for use as a weapon.

Their brave stand turned the tide of battle for the Scots. The old man sank breathless on a stone just as the king came up to thank him. Kenneth asked his name and the ploughman could only gasp: "Och aye"—and that's the name the king gave him—Haye.

Another story has the king cut loose a falcon (which is on the Hay crest) and give the land it flew over to the hero and his sons.

The name Hay, however, is well documented as far back as 8th Century France. La Haye de Puits came over with William the Conqueror and his family eventually moved to Errol in Perthshire, before being rewarded with the lands of Slains, south of Port Erroll, Cruden Bay.

The Hays were also appointed Hereditary Lord High Constable of Scotland, a post which they still hold.

Originally, the first Slains Castle was placed between Collieston and Whinnyfold. There is still a small part of it left. Unfortunately for the Hays, they remained Catholics when most of Scotland, including King James VI, were fervent Protestants. James resented the efforts of the Earl of Errol to convert him to the Auld Faith, and determined to root him out by blowing up the ancient castle.

The Hays didn't disappear from the scene, however, but moved up the coast and built a new castle at Wardhill of Cruden. Fortune smiled on them and they went from strength to strength, until William George Hay, the 18th Earl of Errol married the daughter of King William IV and greatly enlarged the second—or new—castle in 1830.

A series of misfortunes then caused the Hays to fall on hard times, and in 1916 the new castle and its contents were put up for sale. The castle itself was sold to Sir John Ellerman of the well-known shipping and travel company. He in turn gave it up in 1925 and the roof was removed to avoid paying rates. Nature and others completed its ruin.

So that's why Slains is as it appears in this photograph—and all in just over 60 years. As the poet Shelley laments: "when will return the glory of your prime? No more—oh, never more!"

Slains Castle ... most of it dating from 1830. The 18th Earl married the daughter of King William IV.

BEHIND THE FACADE

The decision of Grampian Police calling on the district council to close the Aberdeen City Centre churchyard at 6pm nightly is sad indeed.

In the words of the police superintendent: "It is a shame we have to resort to this action as it is one of the last city centre green areas."

How apt is the police description. The graveyard of the kirk of St Nicholas along with Union Terrace gardens have long been the lungs of the city centre and popular spots for workers and visitors alike.

The great classical screen along the south front of the churchyard and bordering on Union Street makes a pleasing break in the continuous line of commercial buildings and modern shop fronts on this side of Aberdeen's main street. A style of building which even 150 years ago was being compared "with the best streets of any city in the Kingdom".

John (Tudor Johnny) Smith, the first city architect was responsible in 1830 for the design, as he was for many of Aberdeen and the North-east's finest buildings. But the finished work could have been even more grandiose as it was a revised version of the original plan by Decimus Burton of a similar screen at Hyde Park in London.

Between the granite columns are very fine cast-iron railings and the whole frontage is a fitting memorial to John Forbes, the philanthropist.

It is ironic that the area which has given pleasure to Aberdonians for centuries is now considered to be "a place to be avoided . . . and crime is common".

For this was the site pre-1829 used by travelling shows and menageries for many years. Wombwell's Circus was a popular visitor, as were the various peep-shows to be seen for the price of a few coppers!

Tudor Johnny Smith died some 20 years after the building of his Grecian facade and is buried just behind it. But before his death he was involved in a controversy over St Nicholas Church itself.

The minister at that time felt the East Kirk was too old-fashioned and argued that a new building was needed. Archibald Simpson, the other great architect of Aberdeen, and a professional rival of Smith, agreed with the minister and thought the medieval structure was unsound. John Smith declared it to be quite safe.

However, Simpson won the day and drew up plans for a new church. Unfortunately, during the alterations many of the ancient monuments were swept away never to be seen again!

Much of Simpson's work was destroyed when the kirk caught fire in 1874. It fell to John Smith's son, William, his successor as city architect to build the present spire to St Nicholas Kirk, behind his father's Union Street facade.

Following the fire, it is reported that a Bible was found in the ruins. Only one text could be read: *"Because ye have sinned against the Lord, nor walked in His law . . . therefore this evil has happened to you".*

One of the last green areas in the city centre.

THE GREEN STEPS HAVE SEEN RED

There have been many changes to the Green (its name coming from the Greengait—road—or the Gaelic for drying place) over the centuries. The King had a palace—if we can call it that—in the area. He left it in his will to the monks of the Trinitarian Order, or Red Friars.

The Trinitarians became a very rich order, getting gifts from various citizens until some three centuries after they came to Aberdeen they owned all the land in the area of Trinity Street, Trinity Lane and Trinity Quay—hence the name of the shopping mall in the area—Trinity Centre.

Although only their names remain, there are a number of interesting links connecting the medieval Green of Aberdeen with the present day. When the Reformation came to the city in 1560 the Trinity Friars' property was seized by the Crown.

For about 100 years the buildings lay derelict. Then Dr William Guild—remembered by Guild Street—bought them and gifted them to the Seven Incorporated Trades. The tradesmen named their headquarters Trinity Hall! The bakers, tailors, shoemakers and the others remained in the old buildings for nearly 200 years. Then, in about 1847 they moved up to Union Street to the south-east side of Union Bridge. In 1964 they moved again, this time to the corner of Great Western Road.

However, if you want to see the Victorian Great Hall of the Incorporated Trades, it still exists in the shape of the Trinity Restaurant of Littlewoods' store in Union Street—designed incidentally, by William Smith who was also responsible for Balmoral Castle.

Another link with the past can be seen just at the bottom right hand corner of the photograph. The fence covers the gap where, for some two centuries from 1600, stood the house built for Andrew Aedie and his wife Christian Guthrie.

David Aedie, one of their descendants, was among the many citizens slain by the wild "Irishes" let loose by the Marquis of Montrose following the Battle of the Hardgate in 1644. Another descendant is Kate Adie, the BBC's news correspondent, whose reporting from all the trouble spots in the world, especially Communist China, has won our deepest admiration over the years.

The steps from the Green have certainly travelled a fair distance—from the Red Friars to Red China. From Trinitarians to Tianenmen Square!

The steps that span the centuries.

BLOOD RED, GREY GRANITE AND A WHITE COCKADE

In this house over two hundred years ago, the Duke of Cumberland, grandson of George I "the wee, wee, German lairdie", stayed in Aberdeen for the first and last time.

Duke William was in the city on military business—he was pursuing Bonnie Prince Charlie, the Young Pretender, who had failed in his attempt to invade England, and was retreating into the north of Scotland.

Many Aberdonians were loyal Jacobites and were disappointed in 1745 when, instead of the Prince's Highlanders arriving in Aberdeen, there came to the city, General Sir John Cope. He camped his army on the Doo-cot Brae which, at that time, overlooked the Hardgate and Windmill Brae—then the main road into Aberdeen.

In case you've never heard of Doo-cot Brae, it was at the corner of Union Terrace and Union Street, now occupied by a well-known insurance company and familiar to many courting Aberdonians as —The Monkey Hoose.

Cope was later defeated at Prestonpans and the local Jacobites took over the city. But not for too long. At the end of February 1746, the Duke of Cumberland entered Aberdeen with a very large government army. He stayed in Provost Skene's House, situated in the Guestrow, a street which now only exists in name.

The Duke stayed in the east wing, where the main entrance can be seen on the right hand side of the picture. His staff, including James Wolfe, the hero of Quebec, stayed in the west wing. Even after the Duke left, the house was long remembered as Cumberland House.

Cumberland placed his force of 10,000 men in the grounds of the newly-built Robert Gordon's Hospital (now school) which was renamed after him—Fort Cumberland. The stores were kept in St Mary's Chapel, beneath St Nicholas Kirk, while his Mint or Treasury was under guard in the House of the Quakers, then situated in the Green.

The citizens' loyalty to the White Cockade withered rapidly. William was in fact given the highest honour which the city can bestow—the Freedom of the City. His Burgess ticket was presented to him in a golden casket!

On April 16, 1746, the two cousins met at Culloden Moor, outside Inverness. The Jacobites were totally defeated with Charles fleeing for his life.

After the battle the Duke was, for some, a great soldier and a song was written in his honour—"See the conquering hero come". A flower was named after him—Sweet William; the Jacobites promptly nicknamed it Stinking Billy! Most Highlanders remember him however, as The Butcher.

Some older readers will remember a game where boys took long stalks of grass and hit each other with them. The game was called Carl-doddies. How many realise that the game was an re-enactment of the battle of Culloden? The Carls being the Supporters of Charles and the Doddies the followers of King George II. Aberdonians have long memories for some things!

The west wing of Provost Skene's House, with the Mither Kirk in the background.

The part of the house occupied by Butcher Cumberland in 1746.

A GUID NEW YEAR!

Old customs die hard in Aberdeen, but pictured is a tradition which seems to have faded out altogether. Since the outbreak of war, there has been no repetition of very large crowds gathering in the Castlegate to celebrate Hogmanay and to welcome in the New Year.

The painting shown here depicts the locals, and visitors alike, at 10.45pm on December 31 in the year 1887. While in the main the area appears to be the same, there are one or two significant changes.

The statue of the Duke of Gordon in the centre of the square stood on that site from 1842 until it was moved to Golden Square in 1952.

On the left hand side of the picture stand several Highland regiment soldiers—probably from the nearby Castlehill Barracks. Behind them Rolland's Lodging, a medieval building dating from about the 16th Century and belonging at one time to the Masters of the King's Royal Mint which stood in nearby Exchequer Row. Unfortunately, the twin-gabled building was demolished in 1935 to be replaced by an office block.

Hogmanay was the main festive holiday in Scotland, especially here in the North-east. It was then that children received their simple presents to be opened on the first day of January. Christmas was an English custom, which only arrived in this area during and after the war.

The word Hogmanay probably goes back to the time of Mary, Queen of Scots and before her to the Auld Alliance with France—Au-gui-l'an-neuf—New Year with mistletoe.

But whatever its origins, it's celebrated all over the world, in some form at least, and Robert Burns' famous song Should Auld Acquaintance Be Forgot is sung with curious versions of the words, in so many faraway places!

Various rituals are still observed when First Fittin—the person who first enters a house, uninvited, after midnight, should be a man—dark-haired, not flat-footed, or cross-eyed, and should have in his hand a lump of coal, a piece of cake and a pinch of salt. He should cross to the fire (if there is one!), put the coal on and say "Lang may yer lum reek". The housewife is given the cake and the salt to "hansel the hoose".

This is one time when manners come second and ladies do not go in first—especially if you are a blonde or red-head—gentlemen may prefer blondes but not as First Fits!

My mother, whose knowledge would have stretched back to the time when this picture was painted, used to tell me that as children they would go round the doors chanting:

Rise up guide wife an' shak yer feathers,
An' dinna think that we are beggars,
For we are bairns, come oot tae play,
Rise up and gie's oor Hogmanay!

In return they would, hopefully, get cake and cheese slices. Simple days, simple ways.

'A guid New Year tae ane and a' . . . in 1887.

THE AIBERDEEN TOON COONCIL

Many Aberdonians pass the Town House but few have been in it. So we'll push our way through the massive revolving doors in Castle Street and enter the imposing vestibule.

Before us is the statue of Queen Victoria, which at one time stood at the corner of St Nicholas Street and Union Street. As it was made of Sicilian marble it suffered badly from the Aberdeen climate and was moved in 1888 to its present position.

Five years later a bronze statue of the queen was erected on the same site. It was a well-known meeting place until moved to Queen's Cross in 1964.

Circling above the crowned head is the unique staircase. From ground to top floor, neither the steps or the landings have any under support.

When the present Town House was built in 1870, a number of fittings were moved from the previous chamber. These included the Mortification Boards—81 oak panels, displaying the names and often heraldic shields of benefactors to the city, for various charities.

On the opposite wall is the "Provosts' Boord"—a list of each Alderman, Provost or Lord Provost, beginning with Richard Cementarius (the Mason) in 1272 and ending, concidentally, exactly 700 years later in 1971/75 with John Smith (Lord Kirkhill). A new board was then started.

On the second floor is the old Town Hall and Council Chamber. The Town Council met there for the last time in May 1975.

This photograph shows that historic meeting. Above the City Fathers' heads hang the candelabra which were also removed from the Old Town House.

Around the walls are portraits of relatively recent Lord Provosts. These include Sir James Taggart (1914-1919) who was Provost during the First World War and Sir Thomas Mitchell, Provost during World War II. Others are Duncan Fraser—the first Socialist Provost and W D Reid, the last Conservative one.

Included in the photograph are some weel kent faces, past and present. Front left is a smiling Alexander Collie, who later became Lord Provost as also did the then Baillie William Fraser and Robert Robertson, seated top left, to the right of Provost John Smith—the last name on the Provost's Boord.

Some councillors later moved from the Aberdeen District to the Grampian Region—these seen are Eric Hendrie, William Rose, Sandy Mutch, a past convener, and Bob Middleton, the present convener.

Other councillors have steadfastly soldiered on, like Richard (Dick) Gallagher, still to be found sitting in the middle of the Opposition, on the right.

To be Lord Provost is, of course, still a great honour, as Charles Murray knew:

> Nakit tho' we're born, a' equal,
> Honours but wi' age increase,
> Till a Baillie; syne selected
> Ruler ower the Council Board,
> An' tho' never re-elected,
> Ance a Provost, aye "My Lord?"

'The end of an auld sang' . . . the last meeting of the City Fathers in the old Council Chamber.

THE END—CROWNS ALL

On the previous page I wrote about the old council chamber of the Town House, and mentioned the three fine cut crystal chandeliers hanging from the ceiling. I should have added that the ceiling itself is an illuminated record of the past history of the city.

Based on Bishop Gavin Dunbar's famous ceiling in St Machar's Cathedral, there are 84 panels and on each is a shield with the coats-of-arms of eminent people connected with the city by birth, service or education, depicted in bright heraldic colours.

The idea was that of William Smith, who succeeded his father, John, as City Architect. The art consultant was Sir George Reid who, along with William Dyce and John "Spanish" Phillip, must be rated as Aberdeen's artistic triumvirate of the 19th century.

Included among the coats armorial are those of distinguished citizens such as Robert Davidson, the Provost of Aberdeen, who was killed at Harlaw in 1411: The Menzies family who, between 1426 and 1634 held the Provostship an incredible 28 times: Sir Thomas Blaikie, commemorated for his work in modern harbour facilities and remembered in Blaikie's Quay.

William Smith did not forget his father's professional rival, and accordingly Archibald Simpson, Aberdeen's famous architect, has his shield shown.

Also featured are Bishop William Elphinstone and Lord George Byron who was brought up just around the corner in Queen Street and Broad Street.

Next door to the old chamber is the Town and County Hall.

It is shown in this photograph. To the left can be seen the Minstrels' Gallery, and the battle-scarred flags of The Gordon Highlanders are on the right.

At one end of the hall is the rather dark portrait of Queen Anne, painted by Sir Godfrey Kneller. The Queen, who was the last of the Stewart rulers, had 17 children, not one of whom lived into their teens!

Unfortunately, she was fond of a drink and became known among her subjects as "Brandy Annie" for obvious reasons. On her death in 1714, the Protestant Hanoverian George, The Wee, Wee German Lairdie, became king, and James Stewart, her Catholic half-brother, became the Old Pretender never to reign!

A painting of Prince Albert, Consort of Queen Victoria, can be seen at this end of the hall. The artist is the John Phillip already mentioned. Shown behind the Prince, who is in full Highland dress, is the old Balmoral Castle, which was demolished to make way for the present castle, constructed to plans by William Smith in 1853.

Next to her "beloved Albert" is a young Victoria, painted by Herbert Smith. It is said that during the making of Sixty Glorious Years, the classic film of the Queen's life, Dame Anna Neagle, accompanied by her husband and producer, Herbert Wilcox, spent many hours gazing at the portrait to inspire herself for her greatest role.

There are other paintings, including one of the Fourth Duke of Gordon, whose wife, the beautiful Duchess Jean, helped raise the regiment of Gordon Highlanders—but that's another story for another time!

The Town and County Hall. The peak of Victorian splendour.

The Hall bedecked for a dinner to welcome King Edward VII.

Bernard Balfour is an Aberdonian. He is well known as a lecturer, writer and broadcaster on Local History. In addition he has contributed to a number of films and to the Grampian TV series—"The Way It Was".

INDEX

V

W

Y

Z